Home Building Work

Home Building Work

Bill Goodson

Newnes Technical Books

The Butterworth Group

UNITED KINGDOM

Butterworth & Co (Publishers) Ltd
London: 88 Kingsway, WC2B 6AB

AUSTRALIA

Butterworths Pty Ltd
Sydney: 586 Pacific Highway, Chatswood NSW 2067
Also at Melbourne, Adelaide and Perth

CANADA

Butterworth & Co (Canada) Ltd
Toronto: 2265 Midland Avenue, Scarborough,
Ontario, M1P 4S1

NEW ZEALAND

Butterworths of New Zealand Ltd
Wellington: 26—28 Waring Taylor Street, 1

SOUTH AFRICA

Butterworth & Co (South Africa) (Pty) Ltd
Durban: 152—154 Gale Street

USA

Butterworth (Publishers) Inc
Boston: 19 Cummings Park, Woburn, Mass 01801, USA

First published 1977 by Newnes Technical Books
a Butterworth imprint

ISBN 0 408 00276 X

Typeset by Butterworths Litho Preparation Department

Printed in England by Chapel River Press,
Andover, Hants.

Preface

It is not every home owner who wishes to actually build his own home, but a good knowledge of construction techniques and the terms used is invaluable.

An elementary understanding of building and bricklaying can prove very useful when involved in the smaller constructional jobs such as erecting a wall or laying a foundation for an extension. Considerable savings can be made by tackling such work, for employing professional labour these days can be expensive.

The term do-it-yourself encompasses a very wide field of activity and there is much to learn. It is not always easy, but once new skills have been mastered d-i-y becomes rewarding and satisfying.

All the books in the d-i-y series have been written by people with very considerable practical experience and all have been involved in feature-writing for DIY magazine over the years. The authors have also been responsible for dealing with hundreds of readers' queries—which has given them an invaluable insight into the problems encountered in and about the house.

I'm sure you will find their advice invaluable. May I wish you success in all you undertake.

Tony Wilkins
Editor, 'Do-it-Yourself' Magazine

Contents

A BASIC TOOL KIT

Below is listed a good basic kit which will see you through most repair jobs about the house. But you will find many others which can be added as your progress in certain fields. All those mentioned here are referred to in the following chapter.

Surveyor's tape
Builder's line
Builder's square
Wooden pegs
Trowels, large and small
Spade
Ladder
Work bench, fixed or portable
Steel rule
Steel tape
Try square
Tenon saw
Hacksaw and blades
General purpose saw
Cross cut saw
Shaping tools
Wheel brace and set of twist drills
Screwdrivers
Bench vice—can be clamp-on
Wrench
Pincers
Pliers, large and fine nose
Spirit level
Chisels
Masonry drills
Files
Marking knife
Marking gauge
Chain wrench
Putty knife

Nail punch
Bevel
Smooth plane
Brace and set of bits
Spiral ratchet screwdriver
G cramps
Club hammer
Glass cutter
Soft face hammer
Power drill
— plus the following attachments:
  Sander
  Saw—circular
  Saw—jig
  Vertical drill stand
  Rasps
  Flexible drive
  Speed reducer
  Right-angle drive

Integral power tools include:
  Jigsaw
  Circular saw
  Band saw
  Router
  Belt sander
  Grinder
  Floor sander
  Orbital sander
  Planer

Introduction

Whether you are a house owner-occupier or a tenant you should be interested in the construction of your house. If you can use tools correctly and care to study the elements of building, it is possible for you to undertake the small building projects which are described in this book.

The information given is concerned with simple foundation work, concreting, bricklaying, masonry, carpentry, joinery and roofing, as applied in house building. What use you can make of it depends upon your willingness to learn and the skills you can develop with practice.

Always start with something small and simple. Do not be discouraged by false starts. Have another go. Don't tackle more ambitious jobs until you have developed sufficient skill.

Building work which is part of the house and any structural alteration needs official approval before you start. So does any separate structure such as a garage, car port and garden buildings larger than an ordinary shed.

The Building Regulations, which specify requirements for safe and proper construction state that plans must be submitted for approval to the local Council (Surveyor's office).

If in doubt, call at the council surveyor's office. The staff will tell you whether plans and application forms are required. You can discuss the proposal with them, and also ask if planning permission is needed—a separate matter from the Building Regulations.

Usually planning permission is not required for small extensions or garden buildings which do not project in front of the building line and which are required only for normal domestic use. The Planning Regulations are rather complex and it is advisable to consult the Council's surveyor.

The designs and details in this book are generally in accordance with the Building Regulations but there are factors which in some cases may call for modification. Here again the council surveyor will advise you.

You can buy a copy of the Building Regulations and any current amendments from Her Majesty's Stationery Office, 49 High Holborn, London WC1V 6HB. There are branches in several provincial cities. Any bookseller can obtain a copy for you. They are not easy to understand but I have explained in this book as much as is necessary for small home projects.

NOTE

Most of the drawings in this book are dimensioned in Imperial units as they are likely to be better understood than metric units for some years to come. However in the text both Imperial units and approximate metric equivalents are quoted.

It is useful to remember that approximate equivalents are as follows:

$$25mm = 1 \text{ in}$$
$$100mm = 4 \text{ in}$$
$$300mm = 1 \text{ ft}$$
$$1m = 3 \text{ ft } 3 \text{ in}$$
$$1000mm = 1 \text{ m}$$

2

*Showing how part of the back garden can be improved
by laying a mixture of plain and coloured paving slabs
(Edwin H. Bradley & Sons Ltd)*

Chapter 1
Foundations, solid floors and pavings

In this chapter we deal mainly with the use of concrete for floors and foundations of garages and other small buildings. The last part of the chapter details the methods of laying paving slabs for paths, terraces and patios.

Tools for setting out

The basic tools for setting out are as given in the following list.

A builder's line (or long length of strong string) wound on a pair of pointed wood pegs or short steel rods;

A builder's square. This can be 'home-made' of planed wood battens to form a right angled triangle (one side 3 units, the other 4 units and the diagonal 5 units—the units can be feet or metres in the 3:4:5 proportions;

A few wood pegs to drive into the ground when marking lengths or corners.

Other useful tools

In addition to the above you will need the following.

A garden fork and spade for removing surface soil and trenching;

A pickaxe for very hard ground;

A strong wheelbarrow;

A bucket and a watering can with rose outlet;

A long spirit level and a straightedge of planed wood about 100 x 38 x 1800 mm (4 in x 1½ in x 6 ft).

Materials

Concrete can be obtained ready mixed, either wet in a mobile mixer, ready for placing, or as a dry mix in bags for mixing with water as required. Both these types are more convenient than buying separate ingredients—Portland cement, sand and gravel aggregate.

Ready-mix (wet) concrete can be ordered from depots in most towns. If you state the dimensions of the work and the purpose and date required, the supplier will quote for the quantity needed. Take care not to order more at a time that you can place in an hour or two, as cement mixes start setting with an hour.

Dry mix concrete (dry cement, sand and gravel aggregate) can be bought in paper bags from most DIY shops, for mixing with water on the site. This is especially convenient for small jobs or for larger jobs which cannot be finished within a few hours as you can mix the material with water as and when needed. There are several brands which are readily available. A suitable type is Marley mix No. 2.

If desired separate ingredients can be bought. This is the cheapest way if you can obtain supplies of suitable washed sand and washed gravel or crushed stone in your district as well as Portland cement.

Always state the purpose when ordering, as sands and aggregates vary in the range of small and coarse particles. For foundations under walls a high proportion of coarse material is suitable. For thin pavings or slabs, finer material is needed. Specify all sand and aggregates for building purposes to be 'washed' as dirty materials can cause trouble.

Garden stones (flints) and broken bricks, washed, can be used in foundation concrete. Clinkers and ashes should not be used.

Mixing concrete

Concrete suitable for foundations, garage and other thick solid floors and drives may consist of

1 part Portland cement;
2½ parts clean sand (of normal dampness but not saturated);
4 parts coarse aggregate.

The above measured by volume, using a clean bucket or bottomless 'box' which can stand on a clean paving or platform.

All-in aggregate or ballast is a cheaper alternative to separate sand and gravel. It consists of both materials as the aggregate is taken from a quarry of sandy gravel. It can be used in ordinary foundations and as over-site concrete under timber floors but it is not suitable for work needing consistent strength. For paths, pools, steps and slabs less than 73 mm (3 in) thick use a fairly strong concrete:

1 part Portland cement;
2 parts clean sand of normal dampness;
3 parts clean coarse aggregate of maximum size 10 mm (³⁄₈ in).

If you want a smooth surface, for screeding (surfacing) concrete floors and paths, or for making thin slabs use a mix of concrete and sand only:

1 part Portland cement;
3 or 4 parts clean sand, graded from fine to coarse.

Mixing the ingredients for concrete is important as improper mixing may result in loss of strength. The sand and coarse aggregate should first be thoroughly mixed in the dry state on a clean surface, turning it over repeatedly with the spade to make an even distribution of the two materials. Then add the correct proportion of Portland cement and again mix thoroughly in the dry state.

Form a hollow in the top of the heap and add clean water through the rose of a watering can, rather slowly, stopping to occasionally turn the heap with the spade to ensure even absorption of the water. If you add all the water at one go without mixing it in, the cement will be washed out. The aim of mixing is to coat each piece of aggregate or ballast with a coat of cement-sand.

Most beginners tend to add too much water and this makes a weak concrete, tending to uneven mixing and causing excessive shrinkage when the concrete is placed. Mixing should be thorough to give a rather stiff concrete.

Another common fault is to use too much cement under the impression that it will make a very strong concrete. The richer the concrete in cement the greater the tendency to crazing and cracking through excessive shrinkage. The proportions already given are adequate for the purposes stated.

For most purposes ordinary Portland cement is suitable. It should be fresh and, if stored, should be in a dry place. If a bag is opened and left for some time the cement will absorb atmospheric moisture and will partly set into lumps. If it is in this state, it should be discarded.

Foundations

Any building, even a garden shed, needs a firm foundation. The type of foundation depends on the load and the nature of the ground or subsoil.

Strip foundations consist of concrete placed in a strip at the bottom of a trench. The strips must be deep enough to be beyond the disturbance through shrinkage and swelling which may be caused by drying out and cracking of the subsoil in a drought, or by uneven bearing value of the subsoil which may be strong in one place and weak in another.

Subsoils vary widely in strength and resistance to weather changes. Compact gravel or sandy gravel is well drained by its nature and if it is not on a steep hill a minimum trench depth of 450 mm (18 in) is usually sufficient for small houses. Chalky ground varies but if it is well drained a depth of 600 mm (2 ft) may be sufficient. Where the ground is liable to saturation greater depth may be necessary.

Clays are variable in nature. but they are all liable to shrinkage in drought. Local practice is the best guide—trench depths of between 600 mm (2 ft) and 1000 mm (3 ft 3 in) may be regarded as a normal range according to the depth to which shrinkage

fissures may open in a drought. In some cases even greater depths may be needed. The local council surveyor can tell you what depths are suitable.

You may wonder if such depths are necessary for small buildings such as garden sheds, summer houses, home workshops and prefabricated room extensions and con-servatories. For garden sheds or similar structures you can afford to take a slight risk. A trench depth of 300 mm (1 ft) may be sufficient on compact, well-drained ground. However, if a solid floor is also required it is economical to form this as a raft, as described later. This forms a foun-dation and floor combined.

You can make a rough investigation of your subsoil by digging a few trial holes. The surface soil is usually loose garden soil and this should be removed from the whole area of the building. It may be anything

The string line is passed around the corner pegs—it must be kept level. The square corners can be formed by the 3:4:5 method, using any convenient units of measurement or by using a large wooden square

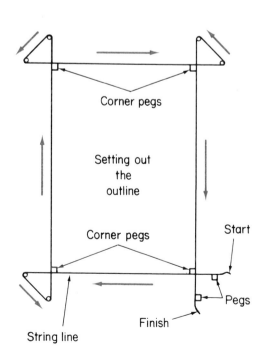

Corner pegs

Setting out
the
outline

Corner pegs

Start

Pegs

Finish

String line

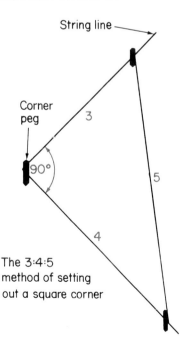

String line

Corner
peg

3

90°

5

4

The 3:4:5
method of setting
out a square corner

from about 75 mm (3 in) to 300 mm (12 in) deep and if it is rich soil it can be spread over the garden. Then, excavate the trench until you have a firm undisturbed bottom. You can test for firmness by dropping a heavy post on it, which should make only a slight impression.

If you take out several trial holes, notice whether there is any variation in the nature and type of subsoil. Some sites have been partly filled with surplus soil or rubbish and may contain weak parts which call for deeper foundations than the main part.

If, from this or any other cause, as on a sloping site, the foundations have to be stepped the concrete should be continuous, forming a riser or step from the lower to the higher level.

Setting out

Before the excavation begins, the outline of the walls should be set out on the ground. Start by stretching a string line across the front building line. Secure to a peg at each corner and then stretch it

along one side. Here you must place the wooden square at the corner and adjust the line to make a right-angled (90 deg) corner, unless for some unusual reason a skew angle is needed. Each side must of course be carefully measured, preferably with a long tape measure.

To check for squareness of the corners and trueness of the lengths, measure the diagonals from opposite corners. Both should be the same length. This applies to a plain rectangle and does not include any projections.

I am assuming that you have a plan of the building, even if it is only a shed. If no scale plan is available make a sketch plan and mark the dimensions in figures. This will prevent mistakes or careless guesswork.

By the foregoing method you will have in position the four corner pegs of the building. But you must remove them before you start excavating as they would be in the way. Before removing the pegs set up a

Profiles set up clear of the trench position. Lines can then be stretched to guide the trench and foundation positions. The first bricks can be levelled as bottom section

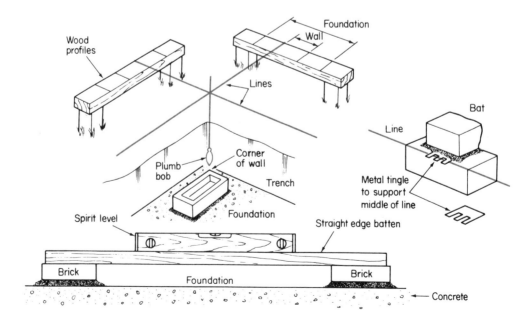

profile at each corner. This can be a horizontal batten marked with trench and wall widths, and fixed on pegs opposite each wall and corner as shown in the diagram. Then, to set out the trenches, lines can be stretched from profile to profile. Each pair of lines allow the trench width for one side to be marked on the ground and trenching can then begin.

When setting out on sloping ground, the tape measure must be held level to give correct wall lengths. If it is held on the slope the wall length will be short. As the level tape will be held some distance above the ground at the lower end of the slope a batten or plumb line should be held truly upright at that end, so that the true measurement can be transferred to the ground.

Levelling

The trench bottom must be levelled. A long spirit level can be used, or a short one placed on a long straightedge (see diagram). If any part of the trench has been carelessly excavated deeper than required, the depression should be left to be filled with the foundation concrete and *not* filled with earth as this would form a soft spot.

If you come across a weak patch in part of the trench you should excavate deeper, if it is definitely soft. But if there are several soft patches of limited extent it is advisable to reinforce the concrete foundation with a pair of 10 mm ($^3/_8$ in) mild steel rods.

If on sloping ground, the strip foundation must be stepped, as already mentioned. The trench bottoms should be stepped so that the minimum depth of the foundation will be as specified. It follows that most of the foundation must be deeper than specified.

Wood pegs should be driven into the trench bottom at intervals of about 1800 mm (6 ft), with the peg tops levelled above the trench bottom by thickness of the concrete required. By placing a long straightedge batten from peg to peg the concrete can be finished level as it proceeds.

Shallow trenches in reasonably firm ground do not need side support. But in soft ground or fine sand it may be necessary to support the sides by placing thick boards and wedging stout cross timbers across the trench to hold the boards against the pressure of the earth. Deep trenches should be carefully timbered and shored; so should excavations for basements.

A strip foundation in a trench, and the sequence of building up the foundation to dampproof course level are shown in the diagrams.

The concrete which should be rather stiff, should be finished level by spading the surface and then left for a few days.

Forming a concrete strip foundation. If the site slopes the foundation must be stepped as shown left. Depth can be measured as shown right

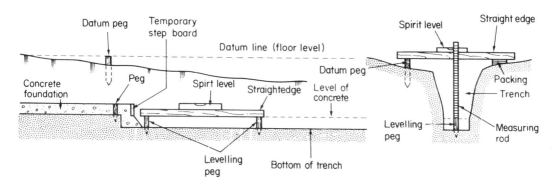

8

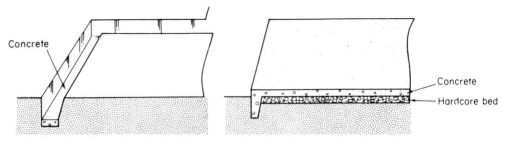

This is a strip foundation in a trench

This is a raft foundation on the surface

Concrete

Concrete
Hardcore bed

Left, the concrete strip foundation is suitable for most walls. Right, the raft foundation is suitable where a solid floor is required or where the ground is soft

Below, the sequence of levelling the foundation and starting a single brick wall

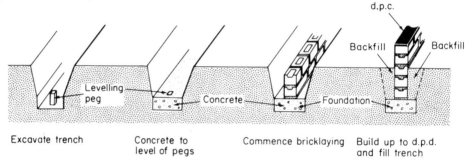

Excavate trench

Concrete to level of pegs

Commence bricklaying

Build up to d.p.d. and fill trench

Raft foundations

Concrete raft foundations are economic where solid floors are required, as the raft also provides a floor as a bonus. It also allows load bearing walls to be built directly on the raft. A raft foundation is suitable also for rather weak ground or ground of unequal bearing value.

The surface soil should be excavated down to the firm subsoil. If the raft must be laid on a site which has been filled (the fill material must be well consolidated) the subsoil cannot be reached. A heavy roller should be run over the site to make sure that the fill is well settled.

Where surface soil is removed it will be necessary to fill up with hardcore (broken stone or clean broken brick—but not shale, ashes or rubbish as chemical action from such materials may disrupt the concrete). The hardcore will allow the concrete to be placed at the required level.

The fill should be well consolidated by ramming or rolling. For a deep fill it should be placed in layers or about 250 mm (10 in); each layer being consolidated before adding the next.

To prevent damp rising through the concrete it is advisable to place a damp-proof membrane of thick polythene over the hardcore. If the hardcore is uneven or of sharp edged material, the surface should be smoothed by adding sand or fine grit. If the raft is to serve also as a floor, the surface of the hardcore fill should be carefully levelled so that concrete of even thickness can be added. The perimeter of a raft should be finished with a rib placed in a trench (see diagram) so that the hardcore fill cannot be squeezed out or rainwater allowed to penetrate under the raft.

Concrete rafts are sometimes reinforced with steel wire fabric or expanded metal. This is only necessary if the bearing value of the ground is very unequal.

The thickness of the raft depends upon load and subsoil strength but 100 mm (4 in) is sufficient for light single floor buildings, conservatories and ground floor room extensions. For houses, 150 mm (6 in) to 225 mm (9 in) according to the nature of the subsoil may be required.

Where there is several feet of weak ground overlaying strong subsoil, piling may be necessary for supporting beam or raft foundations for a house. Short bored piles are suitable. Holes about 225 mm (9 in) diameter are bored through the weak ground, with a special type of earth auger, at intervals of up to 3 m (10 ft), and concrete is poured in and consolidated.

On steeply sloping sites buildings can be built on columns of brickwork, steel or concrete, leaving an open space underneath, if this is convenient. Each column must have a square foundation of suitable size to spread the load and to anchor it firmly. The tops of the columns are joined by beams on which the superstructure is erected.

For small garden buildings on sloping sites short piers or columns are often the most economical form of foundation. A datum peg or post should be driven into the ground with the top at the required level so that by using a straightedge batten and spirit level the piers can be built to comply with it.

Concrete floors

A concrete ground floor is similar to the concrete foundation raft previously described. The surface soil must be removed and a bed of consolidated hardcore laid to an appropriate level. The concrete mix should be as shown in the table below.

The concrete should not be less than 100 mm (4 in) finished thickness. In a domestic building, as well as in most others, a solid floor on the ground must be dampproofed. This can be done by sandwiching a membrane of hot bitumen or tar pitch not less than 3 mm thick, or three coats of bitumen or bitumen-rubber emulsion between the concrete base and a fine concrete topping 50 mm (2 in) thick. These bitumen coatings are available as proprietary brands (a typical make is 'Synthaprufe').

Where timber blocks, parquet or wood panels are to be laid on fine concrete topping the dampproof membrane may consist of asphaltic or pitchmastic material in which the wood flooring is bedded.

The dampproof membrane should be placed at a level not lower than the level of the ground or paving adjoining any external wall of the building. It must be joined and sealed to the dampproof course (see page 10) in the walls. The fine concrete topping on the base concrete should consist of the 1:2:3 mix previously described.

	Cubic ft of aggregate per 1 cwt of Portland cement	
	Damp sand*	Course aggregate†
Ordinary for most purposes, nominal mix 1:2:4	2½	5
For extra strength or thin sections, nominal mix 1:1½:3	1⁷/₈	3¾

*Dry sand increases in bulk when damp—the figures allow for this.

†E.g., washed gravel, shingle or strong broken stone or brick.

All-in aggregate (sand and gravel mixed) can be bought from some quarries. The purpose should be stated when ordering.

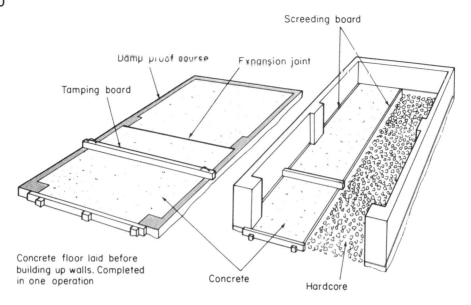

Two ways of laying a concrete floor. Left, at dampproof course level. Right, walls built up first and floor laid in two sections

For a garage or other small floor it is convenient to level off the concrete at dampproof course level.

The base concrete should be swept and if it is dirty it should be thoroughly washed. It should be slightly damp when the topping is applied. If the topping is to be added to an existing smooth surfaced concrete floor a proprietary adhesive bonding liquid should be mixed with a 1 to 4 cement-sand mix, after cleaning the old surface.

To produce a level and even surface, wood battens or boards, the thickness of the required topping, as shown in the diagram should be laid along opposite sides of the floor. Except for a very narrow room, intermediate battens should be laid at intervals of about 1500 mm (5 ft). The trade name for these battens is screeds or screeding battens.

The topping mix should be fairly stiff but must be thoroughly mixed and should be placed within one hour of wet mixing. After spreading about one square metre (slightly more than 1 sq. yd.) a length of straight batten or board should be placed to span the screeds and worked along them to level the surface. A slight tamping action should accompany the movement.

A wide floor, divided by screeds, should have the topping applied in sections, leaving the final section to be completed when the adjoining section has hardened sufficiently to allow you to stand on it. Alternatively, it may be possible to finish the final section by standing on a plank placed over the screeds.

After a few hours, when setting has just commenced, each section can be trowelled with a rectangular steel trowel but this should be lightly done. Too much trowelling draws neat cement to the surface which shrinks when dry and scales off.

The screeding battens should be gently removed before the topping sets hard and, of course, the gaps made good by filling with topping mix and levelling with the flooring trowel.

The topping should not be allowed to dry out during the first ten days. It should be covered with polythene sheeting or other suitable material so that the chemical action of setting and hardening, which can only take place in the presence of water, can continue. It takes about a month for Portland cement mixes to reach nearly maximum strength. Rapid drying results on crazing and dusting up.

Car drives and paths

A concrete car drive may be laid in two widths with a gap between for economy, or in full width. Both these drives are shown in the diagrams. The two-width or strip method, each strip not less than 750 mm (2 ft 6 in) with a gap between of about 500 mm (20 in), can be formed by excavating the surface soil in the strip widths to a depth of at least 150 mm (6 in) and laying a bed of hardcore, well rammed, in preparation for concreting.

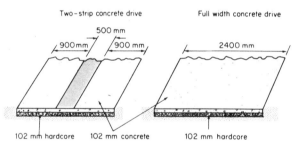

Two-strip concrete drive   Full width concrete drive
500 mm
900mm / 900 mm /   2400 mm
102 mm hardcore   102 mm concrete   102 mm hardcore

The cross section can be straight on sloping ground. On level ground the drive should be cross-cambered for drainage

The concrete should be a nominal mix of 1 cement, 2 sand, 4 coarse aggregate, parts by volume (see page 4) laid to a finished thickness of not less than 100 mm (4 in). The sides should be set out with string lines on pegs.

Side forms of boards on edge secured with wood pegs should be placed to form support for the edges. These should, of course, be removed when the concrete has set.

A thick wood tamping board can be worked along the surface to give an even

finish. A perfectly smooth finish may be obtained by trowelling, as already described, but on a slope it is better to have a slightly rough surface to prevent skidding. Finishing by tamping with the board will then be sufficient.

A full width concrete drive can be formed in the same way. A width of 1800 mm (6 ft) is a reasonable minimum.

As some shrinkage of the concrete is inevitable, long drives should be laid in sections about 3 m (10 ft) apart. A temporary board can be placed to divide the sections—it should be lightly oiled to prevent adhesion. When the board is removed the gap can be filled with sand or cold asphaltic material. In effect this forms an expansion-contraction joint and prevents the formation of unsightly irregular cracks which often occur in extensive continuous areas of concrete.

The concrete should be covered with polythene sheeting, as described for topping, to prevent rapid drying out.

Bituminous and asphaltic surfacing

Bitumen is used to coat gravel or stone chippings for surfacing drives and paths. Asphalt is a bituminous material used as a mix with crushed limestone or grit. Both are obtainable in hot and cold forms. The hot form must be heated shortly before application and is not really convenient for d.i.y. use.

Bituminous mixtures in cold form can be bought and are easily applied. As shown in the illustration a firm foundation or base is essential. This may consist of a bed of hardcore, not less than 100 mm (4 in) thick for a car drive, well consolidated and with the surface covered with coarse sand to fill the gaps between the larger pieces. As the tracks or car wheels tend to form depressions in any but a very firm surface, consolidation

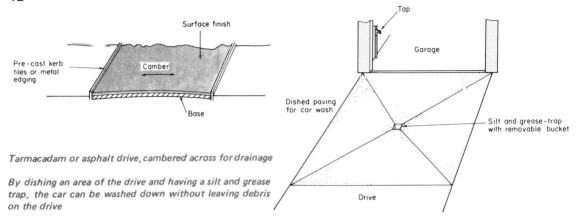

Tarmacadam or asphalt drive, cambered across for drainage

By dishing an area of the drive and having a silt and grease trap, the car can be washed down without leaving debris on the drive

of the subsoil and base by tamping or rolling is essential.

The proprietary surfacing materials of this type are supplied in bags and are simply spread with a rake and then rolled. The manufacturers enclose printed instructions.

A more laborious method is to use cold bitumen, sold in drums, spreading it with a broom over the base and then applying gravel. This is then rolled in and a sprinkling of sand given to cover any exposed bitumen. For a more durable finish a second coat of bitumen followed by an application of finer gravel or grit can be given, finishing with a roller.

For draining water when washing the car on the drive, a drain gully trap in a slightly dished part of the drive, is advisable. This should be fitted with a removable bucket to catch debris.

Paths and pavings

Pavings for paths, terraces, patios and yards can be of poured concrete or asphaltic materials, as already described for drives. On firm subsoil poured concrete 75 mm (3 in) thick is generally sufficient and this can be laid directly on ground which has had the top soil removed and the base well rolled or rammed, but it is better to cover the ground with a layer of sand.

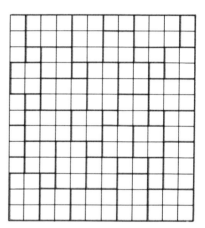

Using 225 × 225, 225 × 500, 500 × 500, 500 × 685 mm

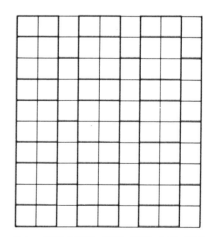

Using 600 × 600, 600 × 300, 915 × 300 mm

Paving slabs set out on a 300 mm (12 in) module, using various sizes to produce interesting patterns. Two or more colours add to the variety. Standard metric sizes are figured here

Bituminous or asphaltic materials should be laid on a firm base of small hardcore or furnace ashes (*not* domestic fire ashes) at least 2 in thick.

The paths or other areas should be set out with string lines and pegs. If a curved path is wanted use a rope or clothes line and adjust it until you are satisfied with the curve as viewed from various angles. Then the two edge lines can be incised on the ground with a pointed rod or a spade.

Paving slabs or flags of pre-cast concrete or natural stone are more attractive than poured concrete or asphaltic materials in a garden. They also have the advantage of allowing easy removal if alterations are required later.

As the natural grey colour of ordinary concrete slabs is rather monotonous it is advisable to buy slabs of two or more colours. These are made by adding special pigments to the mix.

Two or more sizes of slabs allow various attractive patterns to be formed as shown. The following are stock sizes, the larger ones 50 mm (2 in) thick and the smaller 38 mm (1½ in):

Large	915 mm x 600 mm	(3 ft x 2 ft)	
	600	x 600	(2 ft x 2 ft)
	600	x 458	(2 ft x 1 ft 6 in)
Small	300	x 300	(12 in x 12 in)
	300	x 150	(12 in x 6 in)

Laying paving slabs

There are several methods of laying paving slabs. With all methods a firm base is essential to prevent uneven settlement. Soft surface soil should be excavated, and the excavation should be levelled, or graded to an even slope. With a wide area such as a patio, surface drainage is important, especially if the area adjoins the house wall. A slight even fall away from the house wall of, say, 25 mm (1 in) in 3 m (10 ft) is sufficient. Use a straightedge batten and a spirit level and drive a few wood pegs along the outer edge, with the tops lower than the wall edge by the required amount. You can either drive a line of pegs at the higher (wall) edge or mark the higher level along the wall.

After excavating the top soil, a bed of boiler ashes or small gravel about 50 mm thick should be raked to an even surface and then tamped or rolled, if you have rather weak subsoil. Even if you have firm clay this bed will give drainage for any rainwater penetrating the joints as well as providing a suitable bed for laying the slabs.

On a subsoil, such as firm but fine earth or sandy gravel, it is sufficient to spread about 25 mm of sharp sand or ashes, raked evenly, over the excavation. Really fine earth, riddled to eliminate stones, will serve the same purpose.

On such a prepared bed the larger slabs can be laid directly, tapping each slab down over the centre. It is advisable to use the mortar dab method—placing a large dab of mortar to support the corners of the slabs. The larger slabs should also have a dab under the middle. Each slab should be tapped down, using a wood mallet. This should be lightly done—heavy blows might crack the slabs or prevent even surfacing.

It is essential to keep the surface to an even plane. A straightedge should be placed over each slab as it is laid to check that it conforms to the surface of adjoining slabs.

The mortar should not be very strong. A cement-lime-sand mortar of 1 part Portland cement, 2 parts hydrated powder lime and 5 parts sand is suitable. This will allow even settlement and avoid the excessive shrinkage which is inevitable with a strong cement mortar.

The joints may be tightly butted, without

mortar between the slabs. If you prefer a mortared joint make it about 10 mm ($^3/_8$ in) wide so that it can be easily filled with mortar. Pointing mortar should be stronger than the bedding—a mix of 1 part Portland cement, 4 parts washed builders' sand is suitable. It should be rammed down the open joint and finished flush.

Narrow joints of about 3 mm ($^1/_8$ in) are difficult to point with ordinary stiff mortar —hence the preference for wider joints. Narrow joints are best filled with slurry, which is cement mortar with sufficient water added to allow it to flow.

Mortar smears should be cleaned off the surface of slabs, especially coloured slabs, before they set. For this, use rags soaked in clean water.

Natural stone slabs should be laid by the methods just described for concrete slabs. But care should be taken to select a stone which will not readily laminate (i.e. break away in thin layers) under wear and frost action. You can make a rough test by first examining it closely—prominent layering or laminations at the edges will be obvious and if the stones are struck with a hammer the surface laminations may break off. Feint laminations and a dense grain indicate a suitable stone.

For paving, natural stone should be about 50 mm (2 in) thick or little more with a fairly regular surface. Large sizes, although attractive, are very heavy to handle.

Large slabs, whether of stone or concrete, are best 'walked' along by lifting one edge and then allowing one corner to stand on the ground while the other is lifted and moved, repeating the movement with opposite corners. On reaching the laying position the lower edge can be adjusted to the required position and the slab then gently lowered. Slight adjustment can be made by levering. By this method you need not lift and carry the whole slab.

Brick paths

Bricks are excellent for paths and pavings provided they are of dense hard texture. Common bricks and the cheaper facings are not suitable as they tend to flake and crumble under frost action. Bricks can be laid on edge, or flat if they have no frog (depression), in any kind of bond or pattern, in square or herringbone arrangements.

As bricks are small units they should be laid on a bed of thick mortar—at least 25 mm (1 in)— of 1 part Portland cement to 4 parts builders' sand. If the ground under is soft or liable to shrinkage it is advisable to lay a

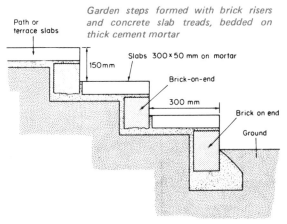

Garden steps formed with brick risers and concrete slab treads, bedded on thick cement mortar

Path or terrace slabs

150 mm

Slabs 300 x 50 mm on mortar

Brick-on-end

300 mm

Brick on end

Ground

concrete foundation at least 50 mm (2 in) thick. The bricks can then be bedded in mortar, both bed and side joints about 10 mm ($^3/_8$ in) thick. The mortar should be rather stiff but thoroughly mixed. Care should be taken to avoid smearing the bricks; if this occurs it should be cleaned off without delay.

Steps for terraces and paths can be formed with half-brick courses for risers, set on end, and concrete slabs for treads, as shown in the diagram. A mortar of 1 cement to 3 washed sand should be used for bedding and the joints pointed. The bricks for risers should be hard, well burnt. Common bricks tend to flake in frosty weather.

Chapter 2
Brickwork and blockwork

In this chapter we cover building walls with bricks and also with solid and cavity blocks. Although the information given assumes you are building a garage or small outbuilding or extension, the principles outlined are equally applicable if you are rebuilding a house or bungalow.

Tools

In addition to the setting out tools—the square, lines and pegs, described in Chapter 1 —the following basic outfit is needed.

A long spirit level cum plumb rule (bricklayers' level) with both horizontal and cross levels, at least 600 mm (2 ft) long.

This can be used horizontally for checking the levels of foundations and brickwork or blockwork courses or vertically for checking that walls are plumb upright, as indicated by the cross levels.

For plumbing vertical surfaces you can use a string plumb line. A plumb bob costs little but any small weight will serve. A snag about using a plumb line is that it is difficult to use in a strong wind. It is easier to use if suspended in a plumb rule with a hole to accommodate the bob.

A bricklayers' line wound on a pair of steel pins is needed to keep courses straight and level. The pins have blades which are inserted into joints at the wall corners and the line is then stretched tight and level just clear of the wall face. Check the line with the spirit level and take care that it does not sag. The bricks or blocks are laid level with this line. If bricklayers' line and pins are not available you can manage with a thin string line and two 150 mm (6 in) nails.

Essential tools for brickwork and blockwork—for setting out, laying, cutting and pointing. A mortar board and bucket for mixing water is also needed. The wooden square can be set out in metric units, if desired, in any 3:4:5 proportions

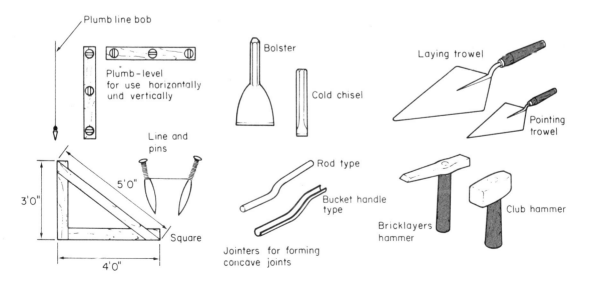

A laying trowel, about 200 mm (8 in) or little more, and a pointing trowel about 100 mm (4 in), a bricklayers' hammer with a flat hammer end and a chisel end, useful for rough cutting; a bolster chisel with a 100 mm (4 in) blade and club hammer complete the essential kit. The pointing trowel is for flat finished joints but it is easier to use a round jointer, producing a hollow finish. You can make one out of a short length of old bucket handle or 10 mm ($^3/_8$ in) mild steel rod, cranked or bent to form a handle.

Scaffolds

Unless you are building a house you will not need ordinary scaffolding, but if you are it may be cheaper to hire than to buy. Scaffolding is of two main types—galvanised steel tubes erected with special clips or joints, and galvanised tubular frames.

The ordinary tubular type consists of standards (uprights), ledgers (horizontal) and putlogs (cross pieces which are supported at the outer end on the ledgers and the inner wall under construction). The frame type is independent of wall support.

Light platform scaffolds for home use are advertised by several firms. These are sectional and are easily assembled and taken apart. They can be used at various heights. The platform is about 1.2 m (4 ft) × 900 mm (3 ft) and is protected by handrails and toe boards. Properly fixed and used these are very safe and although the lateral range is small from a single position, they can be easily moved along.

Ladders in wood and aluminium alloy are made in various grades of strength. Builders' ladders are very heavy to stand up to rough use. Light ladders are sufficient for normal house heights but should be placed on a non-slip surface and, the top should be secured if possible by tying to a window frame. The angle of the ladder should be such that the base distance from the wall is one-quarter the vertical height ground to ladder top—i e., as measured up the wall. If you are working at a considerable height a helper should stand on the lowest rung as an extra precaution against the ladder slipping.

Extendable ladders in two or three sections are the most convenient and the sections can be used separately for short heights. Wood ladders must be stored under cover to prevent deterioration, but metal (aluminium) ladders can be left in the open, although some people find the treads harder on the feet. All ladders should be stored horizontally, perferably on stout wall hooks.

A pair of steps is essential for reaching moderate heights. Here again the choice is between wood and metal. With two pairs of steps of similar rise and a wide scaffold plank supported on the steps at the ends you have a short scaffold though not a really safe one. It is, however, convenient for heights of only a few feet—but 'mind your step'.

Never lean sidewards from a ladder, steps or scaffold. This is particularly dangerous on a ladder as it may slip sideways.

Brick shapes and facings

Bricks are made in a wide range of types, textures and colours, so care must be taken to select the kind suitable for the purpose.

Common bricks, such as fletton commons, are of medium density, suitable for foundation walls, and for outer walls of dwellings provided the exposed surface is finished with rendering or a cement paint or other coloured or white paint. Common

Frog
Standard brick

Plinth bricks

Double bullnose brick

Some bricks have frogs—some not. There are many 'specials'

bricks are not suitable for extreme exposure on both sides, such as retaining walls and garden walls as they may be flaked or crumbled by frost action.

Facing bricks range from mass produced medium density bricks of fletton clay surfaced with coloured mineral granules burnt on to the face to hand-made bricks using specially prepared coloured clays.

The mass produced facings, as made by the London Brick Co. (LBC Bricks), are produced in a range of colours and textures. They are very good facings at an economical price, and are readily available.

Wire cut facings made from coloured clays have a crimped texture and are very good and medium priced. Lime-sand (calcium silicate) bricks are of light colours —cream, pink, white—with several strength grades, some for use in place of clay common bricks and the superior grades for facings. They are smooth and of precise shapes. Concrete bricks are pre-cast and incorporate coloured pigments for facings —they are good bricks but rather heavy.

A range of special shapes is stocked by most leading manufacturers. Examples are: bullnose (one or more edges rounded); bevelled plinths; squints for corner angles of 45, 30 and 60 degrees; sills; copings (half-round and saddleback).

Engineering bricks are very dense and strong. Generally the colours are blues, purples and reds. They are useful for chimney tops and copings and for retaining walls or wherever great strength and weather resistance are required. Some are used for facings but the regular colours and smooth face gives a rather hard appearance.

Brick sizes

The standard brick size in metric units is 215 x 102.5 x 65 mm. In calculating the heights and lengths of brickwork courses the joints must be included. A joint of 10 mm (about $\frac{3}{8}$ in) gives an 84 mm (or 2.95 in) height for one course and bed joint. There is tendency to increase the joint thickness slightly to accommodate slight unevenness in bricks to about 12 mm (approximately $\frac{7}{16}$ in) which gives a height for one course and bed joint of 75 mm (3 in).

The old standard format for brickwork was taken as, to include joints, 9 in x 4½ in x 3 in. The metric format corresponds very nearly to this.

Non-standard bricks are made for special purposes. Small bricks are available for building brick fireplace surrounds. These are hand-made and of various colours and textures. These bricks are also used in ready-made 'slabbed' surrounds.

Blocks

Blocks for walls are of three main materials: dense concrete for external use; medium and light-weight concrete for internal use, and some of medium weight are suitable for external use; clay blocks for internal and external use.

There are several standard sizes of concrete blocks but the most common is 440 mm x 215 mm (17½ in x 8½ in) on the face and with thicknesses of 75 mm (3 in), 90 mm (3½ in), 100 mm (4 in), 140 mm (5½ in), 190 mm (7½ in), 215 mm (8½ in).

The 100 mm (4 in) thickness is widely used for the inner section of cavity walls and for internal load bearing walls, usually in lightweight concrete (load bearing grade).

For the above purposes aerated concrete blocks, of proprietary brands (e.g. Thermalite, Celcon) are now often used instead of the older clinker concrete blocks. Blocks of this type have superior thermal insulation, better dimensional stability and are easier to cut by sawing. If rendered or tile hung they can be used externally. Although the standard type of block is usually plastered inside, a special faced type is made to be left for direct decoration.

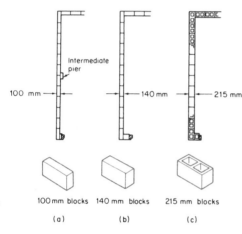

Intermediate pier

100 mm

140 mm

215 mm

100 mm blocks   140 mm blocks   215 mm blocks

(a)   (b)   (c)

Walling blocks are made in several thicknesses—some solid, some hollow. They take less mortar than bricks but most are rather heavy

Hollow clay blocks are made in standard sizes of 290 mm (11½ in) x 215 mm (8½ in) x thicknesses of 75 mm (3 in) and 100 mm (4 in). Plain face for self finish and keyed or grooved for plastering or rendering. There are several proprietary types with special characteristics.

The advantage of concrete and hollow clay blocks over brickwork, at least for interior use where light- or medium-weight blocks are normally used, is that a given area can be laid in a smaller time and less mortar is used.

Stone blocks

Natural stone varies widely in colour, density and durability. As quarried it may be produced in rough irregular lumps called rough rubble. These may look quite attractive in walling but they are laborious to lay and take a lot of mortar.

Regular rubble may be of several sizes but of roughly rectangular shapes and are easier to lay.

Sawn stone blocks are of regular rectangular shapes and assorted sizes. Regular courses can be laid, although each course may be of different thickness.

Before buying natural stone it is advisable to see some walls built of similar material— notice how it looks and how it has weathered. Stone which crumbles or flakes when weathered should be avoided.

Reconstructed stone

Blocks of reconstructed stone incorporate crushed natural stone as the main aggregate, with white or coloured cement. Several firms advertise such material for walling. Durability is usually better than natural stone. There is a range of sizes but for home use it is advisable to use the smaller —brick size or a little larger—as it is heavy material. Both smooth and textured surfaces are available.

Coloured concrete blocks are made of ordinary concrete coloured with pigments. They are inferior in appearance to reconstructed stone but their durability is good.

Split concrete blocks, made with stone aggregates, have an attractive outer irregular surface with the aggregate exposed.

Pierced ornamental blocks or pre-cast coloured concrete are made by several firms for building garden walls and screen walls. The manufacturer's printed instructions should be followed regarding laying, maximum heights, lengths and where piers are necessary.

Mortars

There are several mortar mixes but for home use only two need be considered.

Cement mortar of 1 part Portland cement to 3 or 4 parts builders' washed sand makes a strong mortar suitable for retaining walls and for garden walls if they are of strong dense facing bricks. The admixture of a little plasticising liquid is advisable as it will make the mortar easier to work. For a small job you can use washing-up liquid, but plasticising liquid can be bought from builders' merchants.

Strong cement mortar should not be used for house walls or any buildings of soft or medium density bricks as it has rather high shrinkage which may cause crazing or cracking of the bricks or joints.

Cement-lime mortar of 1 part Portland cement, 1 part hydrated powder lime and 5 or 6 parts of washed builders' sand is strong enough for ordinary brickwork.

Dry mix mortars in bags can be bought at d.i.y. shops and builders' merchants. There are two types—cement mortar and bricklaying mortar (this is a cement-lime-sand mix). For most home jobs, dry mixes are the most convenient buy as the contents are ready for mixing with water and are of consistent proportions. There are several proprietary brands, including Marleymix No. 3 cement mortar and No. 4 bricklaying mortar. As the ingredients tend to separate in the bag they should be well mixed in the dry state before adding water.

Mixing mortar

If separate ingredients are bought, the proportions can be measured by volume, as previously specified, using a bucket or box. The sand should be placed on clean dry paving or, better, a clean boarded platform. Add the cement, for a mortar without lime, and mix dry. Hollow the mound and add clean water through a rose, mixing thoroughly with the spade. Beware of adding too much water. You want a fairly stiff but workable mix. A sloppy mortar will spill down the wall and also tend to crack.

Separate ingredients for a cement-lime-sand mortar should be mixed as follows. The hydrated powder lime should first be soaked in a bucket overnight. Next day the surplus water should be poured away leaving soft lime putty. Mix this with the sand in the proportions already specified to make what is called coarse stuff. Then take enough coarse stuff and mix with the proportion of cement, add just sufficient water to give a workable but fairly stiff mortar when thoroughly mixed.

A cement-lime-sand mortar is 'buttery' and easy to work off the trowel. The strength depends almost solely upon the cement, so it is essential to use fresh Portland cement which has not absorbed atmospheric moisture.

For stonework masonry a similar 1:1:6 cement-lime-sand mortar is suitable for work exposed outside. For interior work a weaker, 1:2:9 mix, is often recommended. If a dry ready mix is ordered it should be 'masonry grade'.

A cement mortar of 1 part cement to 5 or 6 parts sand can be used for external work but with the addition of a plasticiser, as mentioned for brickwork mortar. For internal work a 1:7 mix is suitable.

Brickwork bonds

Stretcher bond is generally used for walls of single brick thickness. The bricks are laid lengthwise (stretchers) with each vertical joint over the centre line of the stretcher below.

The brick outer section of house cavity walls is usually of single thickness stretcher bond, but sometimes snap headers are used with the stretchers to give a more interesting bond appearance.

Headers are bricks laid across a wall, usually a wall of double thickness—215 mm (8½ in) thick—to bond both thicknesses together. They are used in the following bonds.

English Bond. One course of stretchers alternating with one course of headers.

English Garden Wall Bond. One course of headers to three courses of stretchers.

Flemish Bond. A header-stretcher sequence in every course, the header centred over the stretcher in the course below.

Flemish Garden Wall Bond. A header to every three stretchers in each course, the header centred over the middle of the three stretchers below.

Header Bond. Headers only, used on curved walls where the radius is too short to allow stretchers to be used.

In the above bonds bricks overlap those below by a quarter of a brick length 53 mm (2$\frac{1}{8}$ in).

Corners and stopped ends of walls must have this quarter taken up by a brick bat 53 mm (2$\frac{1}{8}$ in) called a closer placed next to the corner (quoin) header. This must be carefully cut by placing the brick on a firm surface, scribing a line, then placing the blade of a bolster chisel on the line and striking it with a club hammer.

The splayed corner of a wall supporting a bay window is formed by laying squint bricks of appropriate angle.

Care should be taken to avoid straight vertical joints through sucessive courses—hence the need to overlap or bond the bricks.

How to build a single brick wall in stretcher bond. The corners should rise in advance of the main part. Keep the line level as a guide

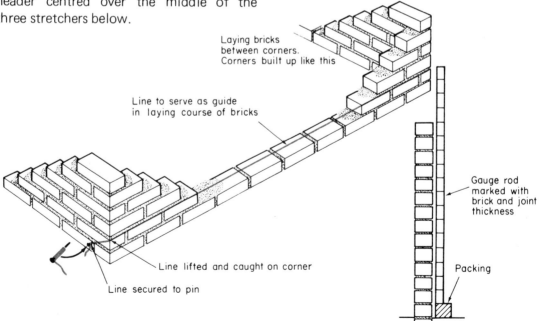

Laying bricks between corners. Corners built up like this

Line to serve as guide in laying course of bricks

Gauge rod marked with brick and joint thickness

Line lifted and caught on corner

Packing

Line secured to pin

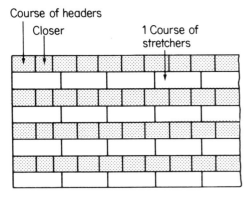

ENGLISH BOND

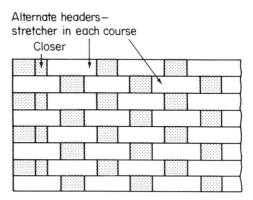

FLEMISH BOND

These diagrams show three different types of bond—English bond, Flemish bond and English Garden Wall Bond

Left, one course of headers in one course stretchers. Right, stretchers alternate with headers in each course Below, one course of headers to three course of stretchers. Notice the closer next to the corner header

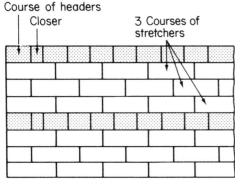

ENGLISH GARDEN WALL BOND

Building brick walls

Brickwork walls for most ancillary home buildings, such as garages, fuel stores, garden buildings and support walls for conservatories and greenhouses, are usually of single brick thickness—102.5 mm (4¼ in) laid in stretcher bond.

With the foundation concrete laid, as described in Chapter 1, place a brick at each corner while you check the lengths of walls. It is advisable to lay a course of bricks dry with a joint gap of about 12 mm (⁷⁄₁₆ in) between them. Then you can see if the length of the wall can be formed without having to cut a brick bat to fit an exact measurement. A slight adjustment of the joint width can be made if the overall fit is not exact. It is useful to plane a piece of wood to the required joint width for use as a gauge.

A gauge rod can also be made by marking a batten with the course heights—brick height plus one bed joint. Four courses to 300 mm (12 in) is generally suitable.

Commence bricklaying by building up the corners a few courses, then complete the first course along the foundation. Build up the corners again, keeping them a few courses higher than the main part of the wall until you reach the top.

The courses must be kept level. Use the string line, secured at each corner by inserting the pins into a mortar joint, and carefully checking with the spirit level. The spirit level should also be placed on the brickwork occasionally and, if it has cross levels, it can be held upright against the face of the wall at intervals to test for being plumb (truly vertical). Alternatively, use a plumb bob and line.

If you are a beginner it pays to check the work frequently at first and also to

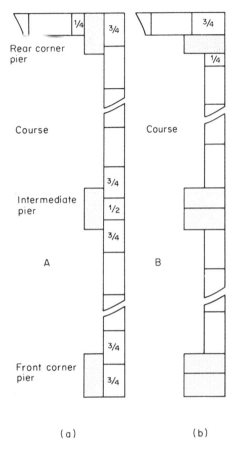

Bonding plans for a single brick stretcher bond wall with piers, suitable for a garage of average size. Course (a) alternates with course (b)

Checking a brickwork corner with a bricklayer's spirit level-cum-plumb rule

stand well back at one end and look along the wall. Any faults in level or plumb will then be apparent and you can correct the work you have done fairly simply. It is only to easy to build a long stretch of wall and then to find that it leans dangerously.

Openings for doors and windows must be left. It is advisable to build-in the frames, placing them in position at sill level and nailing raking struts of timber to hold them upright. Galvanised metal lugs should be screwed to the frame sides at intervals of about 900 mm (3 ft) at suitable levels for building into the bed joints of the brickwork.

Building Regulations

Under the Building Regulations a wall of single brick or block thickness (not less than 100 mm (4 in), must not exceed 3 m (10 ft) high from the foundation. The wall must be bonded at each end and inter-mediately with piers or butressing walls not less than 200 mm square (8 in x 8 in) in-cluding the wall thickness, so that the wall is divided into lengths not exceeding 3 m.

An exception to this rule is where the wall is less than 2.5 m (8 ft) high from the foundation and less than that distance in length. A short garden wall is an example;

Bricklaying to a line stretched and levelled

in such case piers are not essential for strength but may be required for the sake of appearance.

Double-brick walls

Walls of double brick thickness—215 mm (8½ in)—are of course stronger and look better than those of single brick. For work such as domestic garages and long or high garden walls piers are not needed. The English or Flemish bonds, as described earlier in this chapter are suitable—either the full bonds or the garden wall types.

Where facing bricks are used outside and common bricks inside, the garden wall types are economical in facings and of adequate strength. The outside face should be the 'fair' face (perfectly flush) and the inside will inevitably be uneven.

Protecting from weather

Brickwork and blockwork should be protected from hot sun and dry winds to allow moisture to remain in the mortar for at least a week as the setting and hardening action depends upon this.

In very dry weather cover the work with any kind of sheeting as you go along.

In frosty weather, the work must be covered to prevent the mortar freezing and crumbling. The top course should be covered with a plank when left overnight.

Dampproof courses

To prevent damp rising upwards through porous walling materials a dampproof course (d.p.c.) must be built into the wall. This should be at least 150 mm (6 in) above the highest part of the adjoining ground or paving and below the level of the surface of the ground floor (see illustration).

D.p.c. materials of bitumen, suitable plastic, bitumen impregnated felt, or a combination of bitumen and lead, copper or aluminium strip, are flexible and supplied in rolls of various wall widths. They should be laid on a bed of mortar and covered with a second bed of mortar to prevent penetration by sharp corners or grit and to give good adhesion.

In old houses the dampproof course usually consists of two courses of slates in strong mortar. Houses older than about mid-nineteenth century may not have a dampproof course.

Where the ground floor is below the ground level or the 150 mm (6 in) clearance described above cannot be achieved, a

Typical small scale cross section, left; with enlarged detail, right; as for a house. Height of rooms figures are usual but are more than the minimum of 2.3 m (7 ft 6½ in) laid down in the Building Regulations

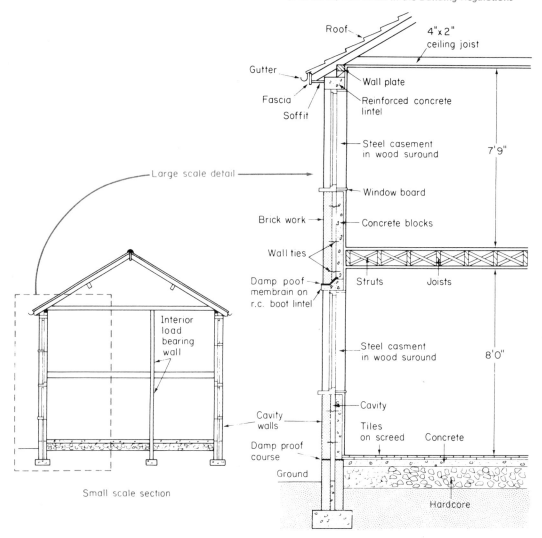

vertical membrane must be placed on the inside face and this must be sealed to the level dampproof course. Three coats of bitumen or bitumen-rubber emulsion can be used for this purpose.

With a solid concrete ground floor incorporating a dampproof membrane, as described on page 8, the membrane must be sealed to the level of the d.p.c. by turning it up if necessary.

Cavity walls

The bricks and blocks used in the outer walls of houses are porous. So solid walls may absorb an amount of rainwater to admit damp to the inside surfaces. The horizontal d.p.c. described above prevents damp rising from wet ground but cannot prevent it passing through the wall.

The most widely used modern method of preventing damp penetration is the cavity wall as illustrated. Normally, this consists of an inner section of 100 mm (4 in) load bearing lightweight blocks separated from the outer single brick wall by a cavity 50 mm (2 in) wide. But structurally the two sections are connected across the cavity by galvanised steel ties built into the bed joints, one per square metre.

Floor joists and roof plates bearing the roof loads are supported on the inner wall section but as this is tied to the outer section stability is assured.

To prevent damp penetration the cavity must not be bridged except by suitable ties and at the top of the wall where it is protected by a projecting roof. In the case of a parapet there must be a d.p.c. in the parapet and joined to the roof covering.

The d.p.c. placed horizontally above ground must be in two separate parts and the cavity must be extended not less than 150 mm (6 in) below the d.p.c. level. Below that, the lower cavity should be filled with mortar or fine concrete.

Building with shell-bedding hollow blocks. The vertical joints should be mortared on the inner and outer edges only. The block should be given several sharp taps with a trowel to settle the mortar and make it stick (Cement & Concrete Association)

The struck joint (Cement & Concrete Association)

As the cavity walls are built mortar droppings may collect on the metal ties and form a porous bridge for water, allowing damp to penetrate to the inside wall face. This can be avoided by placing a batten across the ties immediately below as you lay further courses. The batten can be lifted easily if a string loop is tied to each end, or from corners. It can be withdrawn horizontally if a brick is temporarily left out opposite the end of the batten.

(a) *Reinforced concrete lintel—depth and reinforcement varies with load and span*

(b) *Wide spands should be remporarily supported with a prop until the brickwork above has set*

(c) *Reinforced concrete lintels. Left, for single brick wall. Right, for cavity wall*

(d) *Galvanised steel lintel—made for various spans*

Building cavity walls

When building cavity walls both sections, outer brickwork and inner blockwork, should be built up together. It is risky to build up the single brick outer wall first— although some bricklayers do—as a strong wind may blow it down before the mortar has set.

Care must be taken at door and window openings to avoid bridging the cavity with solid brick or block work. The jambs (sides) of the openings should be protected by placing a vertical dampproof strip of bituminous or plastic material sandwiched between the solid wall sections.

The head over openings should be protected by placing a tray flashing of lead or bituminous sheet over the head, turned up

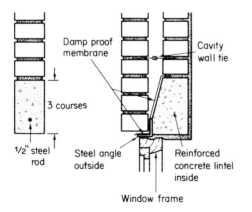

2 courses

Clear span

3/8" steel rod   Mild steel reinforcement

(a)

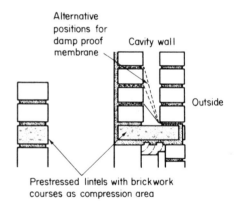

Alternative positions for damp proof membrane   Cavity wall

Outside

Prestressed lintels with brickwork courses as compression area

(b)

Damp proof membrane   Cavity wall tie

3 courses

1/2" steel rod   Steel angle outside   Reinforced concrete lintel inside

Window frame

(c)

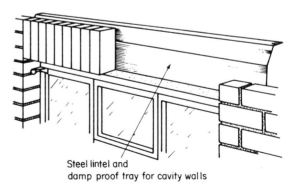

Steel lintel and damp proof tray for cavity walls

(d)

in the cavity and turned at the back into the bed joint of the inner wall section. The tray should project 150 mm (6 in) beyond the opening at each end.

A dampproof strip may be needed under the sill, but where a window frame has a wood sill placed over the cavity this strip may not be needed.

Lintels

Where galvanised pressed steel lintels (beams) are used over door and window openings they form a dampproof tray. Pre-formed plastic extrusions are made for attaching to the jambs of wood or metal windows for making a dampproof closure to the cavity as well as a firm fixing for the frame, so that strip dampproofing is not needed.

Suspended floors

Timber suspended ground floors need under-floor ventilation, usually provided by building in air bricks which also ventilate the cavity. This also reduces the thermal insulation of the wall by admitting cold air to the cavity. It is better to use proprietary plastic extruded floor vents which bridge the cavity but are shaped to prevent water creeping across.

Garden walls

Brick walls for garden boundaries are built in the bonds already described. The illustration shows other typical examples.

Garden walls. Top left, single brick stretcher bond with terminal pier. Top right, double brick in Flemish garden wall bond. Bottom left, double brick wall in English garden wall bond. Bottom right, plans of courses

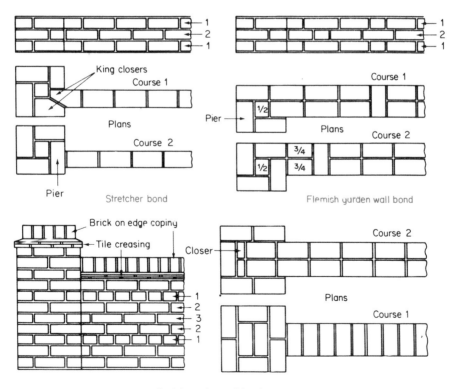

Building stone walls

The methods of building stone walls depend on the shapes and sizes of the blocks, whether rough rubble, regular rubble, large or small squared blocks, one size only or two or more sizes.

If rectangular blocks of a single size not much larger than standard bricks are used, they can be laid as already described for brickwork. Use a level line and pins, and raise it every course, or every two or three courses will do as you gain experience.

Remember that the line must be stretched level and the work checked both for level

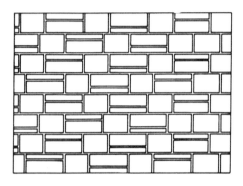

Irregular courses

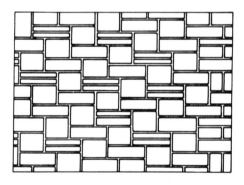

Regular courses

Stone walls. Pre-cast reconstructed stone blocks can be laid in various patterns—these are two examples

courses and for plumb upright faces and corners. The corners should be stepped up a few courses in advance of the main length of wall. Two or more sizes can be bonded as shown.

Blocks of a regular thickness, not less than 100 mm (4 in) thick, can be built in single thickness. If all are of the same size, including length, they can be laid in stretcher bond, as described for single brickwork walls. Walls of double or more thickness, including rubble walls, must be bonded across at intervals of three or four courses. With rough rubble, single bond stones, the thicknesses of the wall should be placed at intervals of not more than 1 metre (3 ft 3 in) horizontally and vertically.

Dry stone walling for garden walls, consists of assorted sizes of rubble. The stones need to be fairly thick, 500 mm (about 20 in), at least for low walls and thicker for high walls. There is an art in laying; the main point is to lay each stone so that it is held tightly by adjoining stones. Gaps can be wedged with small bits. Although no mortar is used in traditional dry stone walling, it is advisable in garden walling to finish the top course or coping in medium strength mortar. Using rough rubble a coping can be formed by laying the top course with the stones upright.

Copings for stone walls of rectangular blocks in mortar are special blocks with a sloping top or saddleback, projecting on one or both sides to shed rainwater. But flat paving slabs, slightly wider than the wall, cost less and are satisfactory on a garden wall.

For parapet walls above flat roofs, as sometimes used around garage roofs, the coping can be of pre-cast concrete saddleback section. Alternatively, you can use a proprietary type of heavy duty plastic or of aluminium alloy, fixed with special clips or brackets. All types are made in various widths.

Sills

If a wood window frame has a sill, as part of the frame, which projects 25 mm (1 in) or more beyond the wall face, no separate wall sill is needed. Some wood frames and also steel frames do not have projecting sills; in these cases a wall sill is necessary.

A wall sill can be formed in several ways, using flat clay roofing tiles or concrete tiles, or standard bricks. Roofing tiles— 265 mm (10½ in) x 165 mm (6½ in)—bedded in cement mortar to an outward slope, two courses to break side joints and neatly pointed, are often used. Facing bricks on edge, preferably a dense type, also bedded in cement mortar to an outward slope and projecting slightly, look attractive and the projecting edge is not so vulnerable to damage as is the tiled type. But there are also special thick sill tiles of clay with a bullnose edge which are bedded as a single course.

Pre-cast concrete sills are made in a range of sizes and sections, all with an outward slope. One type is made for standard wood windows and another for standard metal windows.

All wall sills should have an outward slope to shed rainwater and preferably a projection and a drip groove underneath. The window frame should stand on the sill and it is advisable to seal it with a non-hardening mastic, frame sill to wall sill.

Piers and columns

Attached piers are projections from a wall and serve a variety of purposes. They are intended to strengthen the wall, as for single thickness walls described on page 21; to take a concentrated load, as a bearing for a steel joist; or for architectural effect. These piers must be bonded into the wall.

Columns or independent piers are free-standing and used either for supporting porch roofs; for beam foundations on a sloping site; or for garden pergolas.

Piers and columns may be built of standard brickwork, concrete blocks, or natural stone blocks. The foundation for an attached pier should project from the wall to give even bearing on the ground. For a column, the foundation should project all round, generally to double the width of the column.

Columns or stanchions of tubular steel can be used to support porch, canopy and car port roofs. The base should be anchored into a concrete foundation. For most purposes concrete 300 mm (12 in) square x 200 mm (8 in) thick, deep enough to rest on firm subsoil beyond shrinkage movements, will be sufficient.

Bungalow. Detail at eaves level showing piers at sides of front doorway and wall plate ready for rafters

Chapter 3
Fireplaces, flues and chimneys

A fireplace recess in or against a wall must comply with certain Building Regulations.

On an internal wall the back of the recess must be of solid brick or block not less than 200 mm (8 in) thick, extending to the full height of the recess. Above that level the flue is formed and the solid walls of the flue and chimney must not be less than 100 mm (4 in) thick.

On an external wall the back may be less than 200 mm (8 in) but not less than 100 mm (4 in) thick. The greater thickness is desirable to reduce heat loss through the wall. The thickness of the fireback and any filling behind it must be additional to the above thicknesses.

The jambs (sides) of the recess must be of solid brick or block not less than 200 mm (8 in) thick.

Hearths

The constructional hearth, usually of concrete, must not be less than 125 mm (5 in) thick, extending not less than 500 mm (1 ft 8 in) in front of the jambs and not less than 150 mm (6 in) beyond each side of the opening. A heating appliance for solid fuel or oil which is not placed in a brick or block recess must stand on a solid hearth with sides not less than 840 mm (2 ft 9 in).

An ash pit can be formed in a solid hearth, to hold an ash bucket. This is provided that the solid non-combustible bottom and sides are not less than 50 mm (2 in) thick and no combustible materials, such as timber joists, are built into a wall below or beside the ash pit within 225 mm (9 in) of the inner surface of the pit. Floor joists passing near the ash pit must have a clear air space of at least 50 mm (2 in) between the joists and the outer surface of the pit.

The above paragraph applies especially to solid fuel appliances with under-floor draught.

Brickwork and blockwork for fireplaces, flues and chimneys must be properly bonded and laid in mortar, as described in Chapter 2.

Flues and chimneys

Flues formed in brickwork or blockwork are usually of a nominal 200 mm (8 in) square section for a solid fuel appliance. The Building Regulations require the flue section to be such that it will contain a diameter not less than 175 mm (nearly 7 in).

The gathering which is formed over an open fireplace recess slopes inward from the sides and a throat not less than 100 mm (4 in), but not much more, front to back, leads into the flue proper. The surfaces should be smooth so that the smoke and fumes have an easy run up the flue.

The flue walls should not be less than 200 mm (4 in) thick, exclusive of lining.

Lining

A brick or block flue must be lined with rebated and socketed clay flue linings (or flue linings made from kiln-burnt aggregate and high alumina cement). An alternative

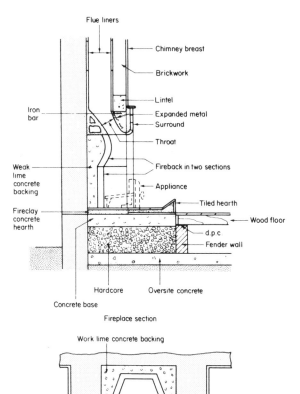

Fireplace section

Plan

Fireplaces with open grate and tiled surround. Manufacturers issue illustrated instructions for fixing

Lead flashing to chimney during construction. The lead is tucked into joints in the brickwork which are then painted

is glazed clay pipes, with spigot and socket ends, socket uppermost. All these linings should be jointed in cement mortar.

There are also proprietary flue blocks of high alumina concrete from which the entire flue and chimney can be constructed. One type is designed for fixing to an existing exterior wall which is convenient when a fireplace is added to a room.

Proprietary flexible flue liners of various types are made for adding to existing flues. These are particularly useful where old flue linings have decayed or where gas or oil burning appliances are fixed in a converted fireplace. The flexible linings can be threaded

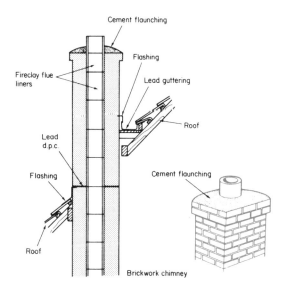

Typical brickwork chimney lined with fireclay liners. The cement flaunching at the top protects the chimney from rain absorption

through from the chimney top. Suitable terminals of asbestos-cement are made for fixing to gas and oil flues at the chimney head.

Outlet

Where a closed stove or boiler of the independent type, whether fixed in an open recess or standing on an open hearth, has the flue outlet connected to a brick or block flue, there must be a small chamber formed at the bottom of the flue. This should be preferably fitted with a small bucket, to collect condensate or debris, and an access cover to allow the bucket to be emptied.

A straight vertical flue is better than one with a bend. If a bend is unavoidable it should be at an angle to the horizontal of not less than 45 degrees. Where flue liners are used with a flue bend, the special bend fittings should be used.

Chimneys

The head or outlet of a flue serving a solid fuel or oil burning appliance must be not less than 1 m (3 ft 3 in) above the highest point of contact between the chimney or flue pipe and the roof, with the following exception.

Where a chimney or flue pipe passes through a pitched roof (a roof with an angle of not less than 10 degrees) at the ridge, or within 600 mm (24 in) of the ridge, the top of the flue (excluding the chimney pot or terminal) may be less than 1 m (3 ft 3 in) but not less than 600 mm (2 ft 2 in) above the ridge.

The top must also be at least 1 m (3 ft 3 in) above the top of any part of any window or skylight capable of being opened, or of any ventilator.

Flues or gas appliances

The Building Regulations relating to domestic gas fires and other appliances are complex. Generally, the printed fixing instructions issued by the manufacturers of a particular appliance should be carefully followed.

Special flue blocks and pipes are made for gas appliances fixed in new houses but flues and chimneys of normal brick or block construction can be used. Adequate air supply is essential for any gas consuming appliance.

The flue outlet must be fitted with a terminal designed to allow free discharge, to minimise downdraught and to protect the flue from debris, and so situated that air can freely pass across it at all times.

The outlet from a gas appliance must be at least 600 mm (2 ft) away from any openable window, skylight or ventilator in any external wall or roof.

A brick or block chimney head should be protected by rendering with cement mortar sloped outwards to throw off rainwater. This is called 'flaunching'. It helps drainage if the two top course projects about 50 mm (2 in).

Flues for solid fuel appliances

With flues for solid fuel appliances a chimney pot is not essential but it may help to prevent downdraught by raising the outlet above the area of air turbulence caused by wind striking the roof or near-by trees. When a strong wind strikes one side of a building it creates an area of pressure but on the opposite it creates suction. If the chimney rises from low down on the pressure side of the roof the top may sometimes be within the pressure area and downdraught may be caused.

If the flue is fitted with clay liners, the

top liner usually projects and, in effect, forms a pot. Round clay pots with square bases are made in several heights. The usual fixing is by bedding in the flaunching mortar but in areas exposed to strong winds it is better to bed the base one or two courses down. With a tall pot this is essential.

Anti-downdraught pots may be necessary in some situations. There are several types but it is advisable to try a metal type which can be clipped into an existing pot if downdraught occurs. A new house in a district exposed to strong winds may have louvred clay pots fitted as the chimneys are built.

Where an open fireplace is to be closed or bricked up, perhaps with an electric panel fire inserted, the chimney top should be protected against rain by fitting a half-round edge tile or a special pot with a ventilated cap. This allows the flue to be ventilated but prevents rainwater soaking down it.

Open fires

The fireplace recess is normally 342 mm (13½ in) deep, front to back and from 685 mm (2 ft 3 in) to 915 mm (3 ft) wide. If an open fire appliance is to be fitted, a firebrick back must be fixed first. This is made of refractory clays which will not readily crack, and there are three standard widths— 355 mm (14 in), 406 mm (16 in) and 457 mm (18 in). The 406 mm (16 in) is most widely used for small rooms. The standard height is 600 mm (24 in).

Standard firebrick backs, which are shaped to include the sides, are usually made in two sections; the upper section having a projecting bulge. This makes fixing and removal easier and also reduces the risk of cracking.

The fireback should be built-in with a weak lime mortar or weak concrete filling, which will yield to expansion and ease future replacement. A mix of 1 part hydrated lime, 2 parts sand and 4 parts crushed brick, by volume, is suitable. This has very little setting strength but good thermal insulation.

Most builders usually support the head of the fireplace opening with a reinforced concrete lintel placed higher up than is needed. It is then necessary to fix a lintel beneath it so that the level of the opening is about 25 mm (1 in) below the top of the fireback, and the back of this lintel should be sloped to form the throat which has already been described. Special refractory throat hoods are made which are better for this purpose, especially where a surround of slabbed tile or facing bricks projects much in front of the fireplace breast.

An alternative to the above methods is to fix a wrought iron bar 75 mm (3 in) x 10 mm ($^3/_8$ in) at a suitable level under the builder's lintel and make up the space above with shaped brickwork. This is not a sound method as the brickwork filling may crack.

The fireback should be set so that a gap of about 6 mm (¼ in) is left behind the edges of the fireback and the back of the surround. This is filled with a weak mortar which gradually cracks and drops out. It is better to seal it with asbestos rope.

A tiled slab hearth and surround may be fixed with the hearth slab tight against the wall and the surround slab standing on the hearth or with the surround slab standing on the concrete hearth (a wide surround may overlap on to the floor), depending on the design. An inspection will indicate which method is suitable.

The hearth slab should be bedded in a lime-cement-sand mortar (see page 19). The surround slab should be fixed to the wall with round-head screws into wallplugs through the projecting metal lugs which are cast into the back of the slab in manufacture. The slab should be placed against the bare brickwork or blockwork and the wall plaster made good to it on completion.

Fires incorporating boilers

There are numerous appliances incorporating boilers both for domestic water supply and for central heating through radiators. Most are totally enclosed—some for building into a fireplace recess and some free-standing. Fixing instructions are issued by the manufacturers.

Fires, open and enclosed, can be obtained with under-floor draught supply and deep ash buckets. These allow better control over combustion and the ash bucket needs emptying only after several days' use. The pipe supplying under-floor air to the base of the fire is connected to an air brick in an outer wall. It is advisable to have two air pipes; for example, one in the front wall, the other in a side wall. This allows for the effect of a strong wind on one wall.

Chapter 4
Small brick buildings

The main part of this chapter is concerned with building a brick garage. First of all, though, we will devote a few paragraphs to constructing a fuel bunker.

Constructing a fuel bunker

With efficient modern appliances and fires for space heating and hot water supply, and the fact that coal and smokeless fuels are again competitive with oil, gas and electricity, the problem of solid fuel storage is still important in many homes.

Fuel bunkers of pre-fabricated concrete sections can be bought and are easy to bolt together, on a slab or concrete base, but the sections are heavy to handle. If you can tackle simple bricklaying, a brick walled bunker may be preferable, and you can choose the size and capacity.

The example is of single brick thickness with a wood top and lid. Inside measurements are: 1 m (3 ft 3 in) square on plan, average height 1.3 m (4 ft). Solid fuels vary in weight from light coke to heavy coal. This bunker should hold about ½ ton of the heaviest and ⅜ ton of the lightest (the Imperial ton is roughly equal to the metric tonne).

A bunker of similar construction could be larger. If the width is increased by half this would increase the capacity by half. If you use two kinds of solid fuel, a double bunker would be suitable—twice the width but with a dividing wall in the middle.

The walls in brickwork or blockwork, at least 100 mm (4 in) thick, should be laid in stretcher bond, building up the corners slightly in advance of the main part, and taking care to level the courses and plumb

A coal bunker with walls of single brick in stretcher bond. For two kinds of solid fuel a pair could be built, semi-detached

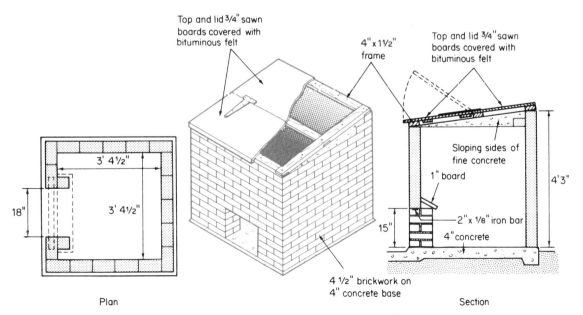

Top and lid ¾" sawn boards covered with bituminous felt

4" x 1½" frame

Top and lid ¾" sawn boards covered with bituminous felt

3' 4½"

3' 4½"

18"

Sloping sides of fine concrete

1" board

4'3"

2" x ⅛" iron bar

15"

4" concrete

4½" brickwork on 4" concrete base

Plan

Section

the surfaces, as described on page 21. A cement-sand mortar; 1 part Portland cement to 4 parts washed builders sand, with a little plasticising liquid added to make it easy to work—as mentioned in an earlier chapter, for a small job like this washing-up liquid will serve.

The sides should be finished to a slope along the top edge so that the roof can slope for shedding rainwater. The top course of bricks can be cut and the roughness rendered smooth with mortar. Alternatively, the top can be formed in cement mortar or fine concrete by fixing two boards on opposite sides, to the required slope, and pouring the mortar or concrete between the boards, finishing by tamping it and finally smoothing the top with the trowel.

When set the top should be drilled to take wallplugs to allow the roof frame to be screwed down.

An opening must be left in the brickwork or blockwork front to allow the fuel to be shovelled out. The brickwork should be returned to form a short pier each side of this opening. Then a 25 mm (1 in) thick board should be fixed on top, sloping a little, so that the fuel is prevented from spilling through the opening. This is preferable to a vertical sliding door.

The roof

The roof frame consists of 75 mm (3 in) x 38 mm (1½ in) timber, fixed with 8 gauge galvanised screws. The frame should be halved (jointed) at the corners, and covered with 20 mm (¾ in) boards. The lower part should be framed as a full width lid, hinged to the upper part with 450 mm (18 in) tee hinges. Roof and lid should be covered with bituminous roofing felt, with the edge of the felt on the fixed roof overlapping the lid felt by about 20 mm (¾ in).

The full width lid can be pushed back to given an ample opening when fuel is delivered in bags

The timber roof should be brush treated with preservative before fixing the felt.

Building a garage

A home garage with walls of bricks or blocks is within the capacity of an experienced d.i.y. family. I say 'family' because if the job is to be done in a reasonable time, you need some help even if it is only fetching and carrying tools and materials. In fact this is the best kind of help because you can then get on with the skilled work.

You should have had some bricklaying and carpentry experience first, if it is only building a low wall in the garden or a timber shed.

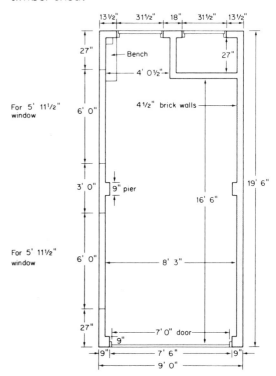

Plan of a garage with a rear compartment for solid fuel, tools, or as a boiler house; single brick walls (or blocks) with piers

The garage can be attached to the side of the house or detached with a passage between, whichever is most convenient.

Plans must first be submitted to the local council (Surveyor's Office) and an approval notice obtained before you start work (see Introduction).

A detached garage

The diagrams show the plan, elevations and sections, as required by the council's surveyor and also as working drawings on the job. In addition the surveyor must have a block plan showing the position of the site.

The plan shown includes a fuel or tool store at the rear. Alternatively, an oil fired boiler for central heating could be accommodated here.

The inside length of the garage is 5 m (16 ft 4 in), inside width 2.5 m (8 ft 3 in). If you have the space it is an advantage to make the garage so that the car doors can be opened fairly wide on one side at least.

The walls are of single brick thickness (or standard 100 mm (4 in) concrete blocks can be used). Projecting piers bonded to the wall must be placed at the front, rear and mid-way along the sides. The front piers should allow for a standard entrance door at least 2.1 m (7 ft) wide. Standard windows of wood or metal can be used. Two wide windows are better than one as you need plenty of daylight if you do any servicing of the car.

The roof is flat in cross section (see diagram), but a fall for drainage is necessary. The roof fall can be lengthwise, as shown, or sideways; not less than 50 mm (2 in) in 3 m (10 ft) is advisable. The floor to ceiling height in the middle should not be less than 2.28 m (7 ft 6 in).

Assuming that the council have approved your plans (in writing) and have supplied notice forms for you to complete and send to the surveyor at various stages of the work (work commenced; foundations ready for inspection; walls completed; roof completed; building·completed), you can order the materials and start work.

The job should be done in the following sequence.

Front section of garage, with single brick (or block) walls and flat roof with back fall for drainage. See also plan and side elevation on pages 36 and 38

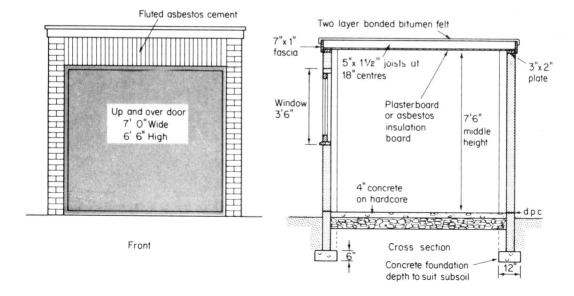

Fluted asbestos cement

Up and over door
7' 0" Wide
6' 6" High

Front

Two layer bonded bitumen felt

7"x 1" fascia

5"x 1½" joists at 18" centres

3"x 2" plate

Window 3'6"

Plasterboard or asbestos insulation board

7'6" middle height

4" concrete on hardcore

d.p.c.

Cross section

Concrete foundation depth to suit subsoil

6"

12"

38

Setting out

Strip the top soil and roughly level it over an area extending about 300 mm (1 ft) beyond the outer line of the walls. Set out the outline with string line and corner pegs, squaring the angles. Fix wood profiles at each corner well clear of the wall corners. Stretch lines all round to give the trench lines— score these on the ground and excavate the trenches to a firm bottom (the council surveyor will advise what minimum depth is required).

The strip foundation concrete can be placed as soon as the trench bottom has been levelled. In most cases a width of 300 mm (12 in) and thickness of 150 mm (6 in) may be sufficient, with projections to take the piers.

If the ground has been filled to a depth of several feet or is rather weak it will be better to have a concrete combined foundation and floor (see page 8). Although the concrete can be prepared by any of the methods described in Chapter 1, the easiest is to buy ready-mix (wet) and prepare for placing it as soon as delivered.

Top, side elevation of garage, with two standard windows (a single window or any suitable type if preferred). Roof joists should be tilted slightly to allow for back fall to roof. Below, cross-section of the garage. See also pages 36 and 37

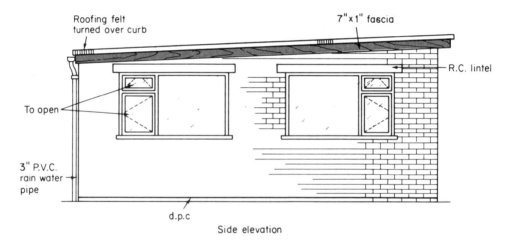

Side elevation

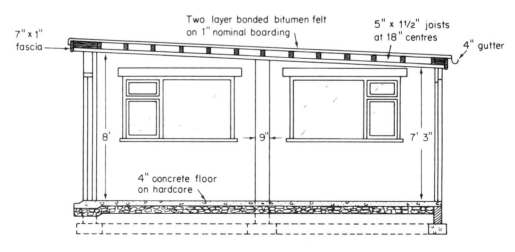

Cross section

Laying the bricks

Assuming that strip foundations have been placed in a trench, the next step is to stretch lines from the corner profiles to the outline of the walls. Hold a plumb line at the corner intersection of the lines to give you the first corner mark on the foundation. Repeat at each corner.

Check the length of walls with a tape measure. Lay a brick at each corner, bedding it in mortar, but then lay one course loose to check if you can fit whole bricks within the length, allowing for joints. Make any slight adjustment necessary. Then the first course can be laid, advancing the corners first, as already described.

The front piers are two bricks square, including the wall thickness. Whole bricks are used in one course but to allow the next course to overlap, three-quarter bats must be cut with the bolster chisel and club hammer. With the intermediate piers, a pair of whole bricks are laid as headers in one course but a half bat and a stretcher must be laid in the next course (See page 20 for details of bonding).

On reaching ground level you must consider where the dampproof course should be placed. It should be at least two courses above the finished ground level or paving but this will bring it above the floor level. Some builders place the dampproof course of a garage at floor level, which may be less than one course above ground. It is better to place the d.p.c. two courses up and then give the inside face of the wall two or three coats of a bituminous emulsion from under the floor level to d.p.c. level.

The door frames

When the d.p.c. has been placed, the door frames should be erected. They can be left until the walling is finished but it is better to build them in as the bricklaying proceeds, so that galvanised steel ties screwed to the frame sides can be built into wall bed joints. The feet of the frame should have metal dowels fitted for securing them to the floor concrete.

Before fixing wood frames clean them up with medium sandpaper, even if this rubs off some of the priming paint. Then give them an undercoat of paint. Also paint the sides, which will be in contact with the wall jambs and the end grain at the feet, with a coat of gloss paint. This treatment will prevent rot starting when these surfaces are concealed.

Take care to plumb the frames upright and to provide temporary struts to prevent accidental movement while the walls are built.

It is usual for the rear or side door of a small garage to be hung to open outwards so that the car can be driven close to it. But if you have enough length it is better to hang it to open inwards as with outward opening the door blows about in a strong wind if left open. So bear this in mind when fixing the frame as the rebate for the door must suit the direction of opening.

For the front entrance door you must have a rebated frame for hinged side hung doors, opening outwards. But most people now prefer an up-and-over door of wood, metal or fibreglass. For this type a plain frame 100 mm (4 in) x 75 mm (3 in) is usually suitable. The manufacturers of this type of door issue illustrated fixing instructions which should be carefully followed.

The concrete floor can be placed either when the brickwork reaches floor level or after completion of the walls. The former is the most convenient as the work can be done partly from outside.

The concrete should be covered with polythene or other sheeting to retard drying out, for at least one week.

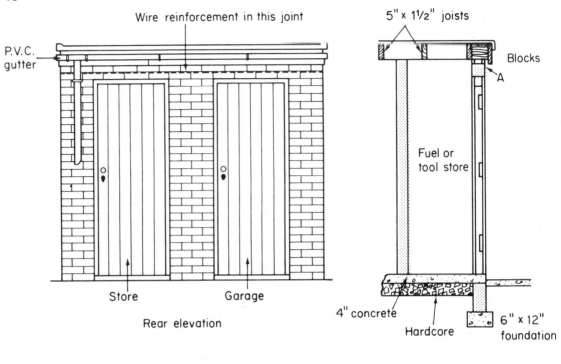

Wire reinforcement in this joint

P.V.C. gutter

Store

Garage

Rear elevation

5" x 1½" joists

Blocks

A

Fuel or tool store

4" concrete

Hardcore

6" x 12" foundation

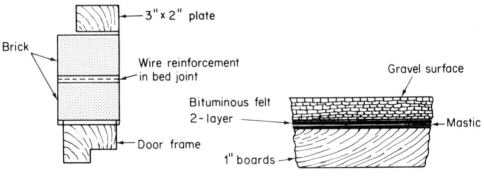

3" x 2" plate

Brick

Wire reinforcement in bed joint

Door frame

Detail of doorway head at A

Gravel surface

Bituminous felt 2 - layer

Mastic

1" boards

Detail of roofing

The window frames

Take care not to go on building complete courses beyond window sill level. As soon as this level is reached place the window frames in position. A galvanised steel tie should be screwed to the frame sides and built into the brickwork, and the projecting ends of the wood sill also built-in.

The front frame can be extended over the entrance doorway so that the space over can be boarded or covered with flat asbestos-cement sheet.

Garage; top, rear elevation and section. Bottom left, detail over rear doors. Bottom right, detail of felt covered roofing with gravel finish

If you prefer brickwork over the front opening it will be necessary to fix a reinforced concrete beam. This can be formed by erecting timber shuttering of thick boards, at least 30 mm (1⅛ in). The bottom board should be supported on stout struts —metal G cramps or short battens nailed across the top edge of the boards. The shuttering must be secure and should not bend when the concrete is poured in.

A 1:2:3 mix, Portland cement—washed sand—coarse aggregate of small chippings (see page 4) is suitable. The timber shuttering should be lined with thin oil or polythene sheeting to prevent adhesion. After placing 38 mm (1½ in) of concrete, the steel reinforcing rods should be placed. Two rods of mild steel, not less than 10 mm (³⁄₈ in) diameter for a span not exceeding 2.4 m (8 ft) with the ends bent upwards will be sufficient. The concrete

should be filled up to make a beam depth not less than three courses of brickwork, 230 mm (9 in).

Alternatively, you can buy a pre-stressed concrete lintel which is only 75 mm (3 in) deep but this type must be temporarily propped underneath while at least three

Garage; detail of front with overhang of roof. Top left, wall plate bolted down to brickwork. Roof hoists are nailed to plates

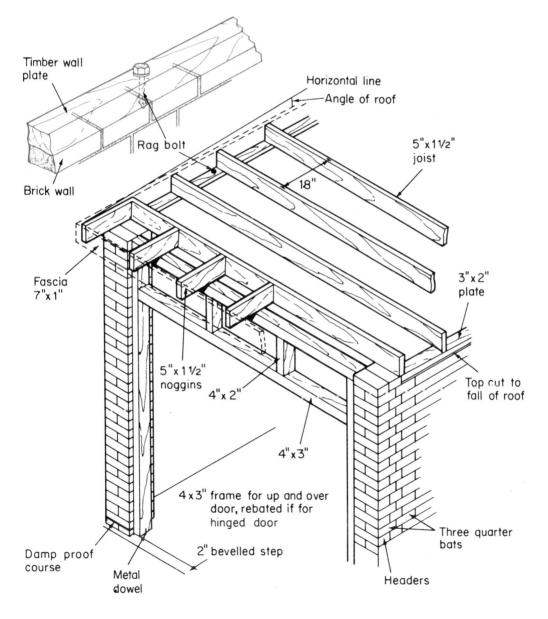

courses of brickwork are built on it. In fact the brickwork forms part of the beam by taking the compressive stress while the lintel takes the tensile stress.

The side windows should also have reinforced concrete lintels if brickwork is built over them. Some builders place a garage window high up and merely nail a timber place over the head. This will serve if no brickwork is built over the opening, though the roof joists must bear on the plate so it should be not less than 75 mm (3 in) thick.

The roof

The roof, as illustrated, projects at the front. As the roof joists are placed across the side walls the front projection is formed by placing noggins (short lengths of offcuts from the joists) and nailing them to the first joist and also to the top frame or plate.

The roof has a fall of about 228 mm (9 in) from front to rear end, as already explained, the side walls must be finished to this slope. The timber plate should be bolted to the wall with three 10 mm ($^3/_8$ in) 150 mm (6 in) bolts, preferably anchor or rag bolts, built into the brickwork. Builders often

neglect to do this but unsecured flat roofs have been known to sail away in a very strong gale.

The roof joists are spaced 450 mm (18 in) centres, nailed to the wall plates. Ends are flush with the outer wall face and are covered by nailing on a fascia board. The projecting front and rear are also covered with a fascia board. Roof construction and coverings are further described in Chapter 6.

The ceiling may be covered with 10 mm ($^3/_8$ in) plasterboard or with asbestos insulating board, using 2.4 mm (8 ft) long sheets, the length crossing the joists. A proprietary filler can be used for filling the joints, using a putty knife or small trowel.

An alternative to a flat roof is a pitched centre ridge roof, covered either with concrete tiles or asbestos-cement sheeting, as described in Chapter 6.

A rainwater gutter, 100 mm (4 in) half round or rectangular section, fixed on brackets, with one stopped end and one stopped end with outlet spigot, and a 3 in downpipe are needed to drain the roof. The gutter should be laid to a slight fall towards the outlet. A string line should be stretched as a guide when fixing the brackets to the fascia. Plastic p.v.c. gutters and pipes are available in most d.i.y. shops.

Chapter 5
Carpentry-floors and joists

Carpentry is the craft of building construction in timber—mainly sawn timber (not planed). In the case of houses this includes timber floors and roofs. Partitions, conservatories, garden buildings and fences may also be framed in timber.

Several firms offer prefabricated houses and bungalows which include timber framed walls. These are made in sections for erection on prepared foundations by a builder or a reasonably skilled d.i.y. team.

Tools

For cutting and fixing sawn timbers few tools are needed. More tools will be required for joinery, see Chapter 6. All woodcutting tools must be of good quality and maintained in good condition for ease and accuracy in working.

These are the tools you will require:

Handsaw, 600 mm (24 in), medium teeth for ripping and cross cutting.
Backed saw, 300 mm (12 in) for cutting joints and accurate trimming.
Portable electric saw (optional). Useful on a big job.
Sawing horse or trestle, preferably two for supporting long lengths of timber.
Claw hammer, large.
Try square, for marking off lengths with square ends.

Rules, folding boxwood, also a long tape measure or flexible steel rule.
Brace, preferably ratchet type, with set of bits or drills.
Electric drill (optional), preferably two-speed type.
Screwdriver, large and small.
Pincers.
Hasp or shaper plane, coarse, for trimming.
Carpenters' pencil.
G clamps, one medium size, one large, for holding timbers in position while sawing or fixing.
Plane, large, required if sawn timbers need to be planed to required thickness.
String line, for setting out and alignment.
Spirit level, large.

Materials

Timber

Most of the timbers used in carpentry are softwoods. Timbers *imported* into the UK are: Douglas Fir, Western Hemlock, Pitch Pine, Redwood and Spruce. Timbers *grown* in the UK include: Douglas Fir, Larch and Scots Pine.

Western Red Cedar is sometimes used for framing conservatories and garden sheds where high resistance to decay is desirable, but this timber is not as strong as the above softwoods. It is usually planed for use and makes very durable exterior boarding, but the natural brown colour tends to fade in sunlight. Wood preservative dyes can be applied to renew the colour.

Hardwoods are not much used in carpentry but where ceiling joists are exposed, oak or one of the imported hardwoods may be used for the good appearance, at considerable extra cost.

Carpentry timbers should be straight and free from large defects such as loose knots, shakes or deep fissures. Although as sent from the timber conversion yards they may be properly seasoned, hardwoods may absorb excessive moisture if left in the open. They should be stored under cover but well ventilated by separating them with slips of thin wood.

Softwoods can be impregnated with chemicals to give high resistance against dry rot, insect attack and fire. Hardwoods such as oak and iroko have some natural resistance to fire. Impregnated timber can be ordered through most main timber suppliers at an extra cost of about 15 per cent.

Brush application of preservatives, such as creosote, gives temporary protection to softwoods. However penetration is not deep and the treatment must be renewed every two years or so if the timber is exposed to damp conditions.

In some areas in the south of England, preservative treatment of structural softwoods is compulsory owing to the prevalence there of wood-boring insects. The local council surveyor will give advice on this.

To avoid dry rot, structural timbers must be continuously ventilated and protected from damp. Hence, air bricks are used to ventilate the under-floor space of ground floors of timber and it is necessary to protect joists from rising damp by placing them above a dampproof course.

In damp stagnant air the fungus spores of dry rot quickly develop and destroy the timber. Such timber should be removed and burnt.

Nails

In carpentry, steel round wire or oval nails are generally used for fixing one timber to another. The round-head wire nail is used for most work but the oval nail has a neater head which can be punched in if desired. The lost-head nail is easier still to punch in.

For fixing joints and roof timbers, wire nails 100 mm (4 in), 125 mm (5 in) and 150 mm (6 in) are suitable, but smaller sizes are made. All are sold by weight.

Screw nails have a spiral twist running the full length. They have superior holding power against withdrawal stresses.

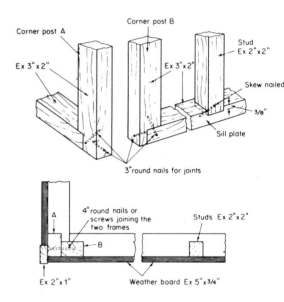

Simple framing joints. These joints are suitable for substantial sheds and conservatories. The frames can be sectional, the corners being joined A to B by screwing or nailing

Screws

Although not much used in carpentry, screws are sometimes an advantage for superior holding power or where in an existing structure heavy hammering might damage ceilings. A hole should be drilled slightly smaller than the maximum diameter of the screw thread.

Nails and screws used in exterior positions exposed to the weather should be galvanised or of rustproof metal to avoid rapid corrosion.

Simple framing joints, secured by nailing, are illustrated.

For heavy loads, bolts can be used, either alone or with timber connectors. There are several types. The coach screw-bolt is a stout screw, one end pointed and the other square headed so that it can be screwed into a hole of appropriate diameter with a spanner. This type is used where it would not be possible to pass a bolt right through the two timbers.

The ordinary coach bolt has a square nut and a round head. It is made in a range of sizes but, for most carpentry uses 10 mm ($^3/_8$ in) diameter bolts are adequate. A washer should be placed behind the nut.

The stress transmitted to the timber fibres by a bolt is concentrated on a rather small area. So for heavy loads a timber connector, square or round, is placed between the two timbers and the bolt then tightens the connector which transmits much of the stress over a wider area. Bolts and timber connectors are often used in roof trusses to joint overlapping timbers.

Jointing plates

Nail plates form another type of joining device for light roof trusses and frames. They consist of steel plate with a series of nail holes to take comparatively small 50 mm (2 in) nails.

Spiked plates have integral spikes similar to nails but they cannot be hammered in. They are forced in with a special compression tool and are used mainly in the manufacture of prefabricated roof trusses.

Timber floors

Timber floors consist of floor joists and floorboards or panels. A ground floor of this type is called a suspended floor because it is supported at the ends; and, for a wide floor, at intermediate positions, usually on sleeper walls with timber plates placed on a dampproof course (see illustrations).

The Building Regulations require a space height from the over-site concrete to the underside of the floor joists of not less than 125 mm (5 in). This space must be clear of debris and ventilated (usually by air bricks in the outer walls and honeycomb construction in the sleeper walls).

As a precaution against rot it is advisable to give a generous brush coating of preservative to the ends of the floor joists. This treatment should extend 300 mm (1 ft) the joist.

A timber joist ground floor must be ventilated underneath through air bricks. Where a timber joist floor adjoins a solid concrete floor, pipes must be laid to allow through ventilation

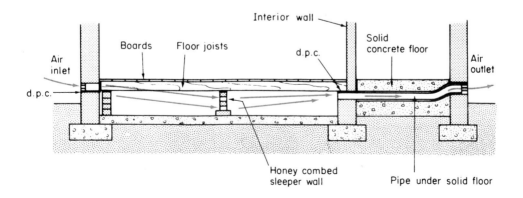

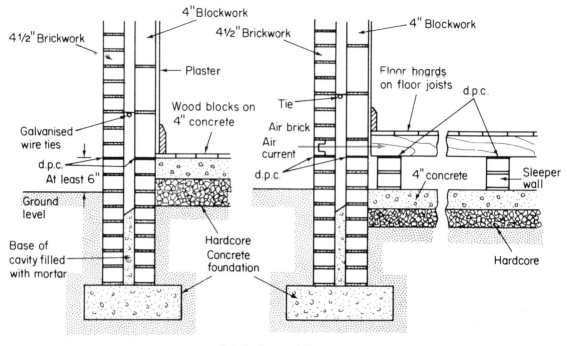

Detail of ground floors
against cavity walls

Upper floors of timber joist construction also serve as ceiling joists. In small houses these joists span between opposite load-bearing walls—from an outer wall to an inner dividing wall, or between two inner dividing walls. For exceptionally wide spans it is economical to use rolled steel

Detail of ground floors against cavity walls. Left, solid floor. Right, timber joist floor. Notice positions of dampproof courses and the dampproof membrane in the solid floor

Galvanised steel joist hangers. Left, hooked over a timber beam. Right, built into brickwork bed joint

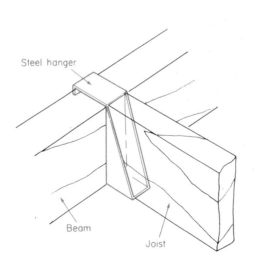

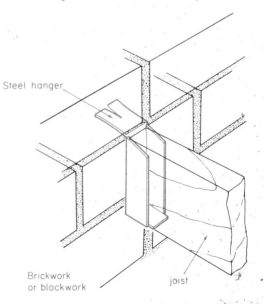

beams to give intermediate support to the floor joists. The steel beams must be cased in incombustible material, such as plasterboard.

With cavity outer walls, the joist end is built into the inner section of the wall. It should not project into the cavity as, if it does, mortar droppings might lodge there and form a bridge for moisture to cross the cavity (see page 25).

Steel joist hangers are convenient for supporting upper floor joists on beams or walls.

Floor joist sizes

Timber floor joists for domestic buildings must be selected for size according to the spacing and floor load. This data is tabulated in the Building Regulations. Depths of joists range from 75 mm (3 in) to 225 mm (9 in); thicknesses from 38 mm (1½ in) to 75 mm (3 in). These are nominal standard sizes, as sawn.

Standard spacings, centre to centre, are 400 mm (16 in) and 450 mm (18 in), for tongued and grooved floorboards of not less than finished thickness 16 mm (approximately $2\frac{1}{32}$ in).

The table shows standard spacings for the 38 mm (1½ in) thickness, usually the most economical to use.

This table applies only to normal domestic floor loads and where the dead loads (weight of flooring excluding the joists) and any partitions or other structural loads supported on the floor do not exceed 25 kilogrammes per square metre (5lb per sq. ft.) The Building Regulations should be consulted for dead loads exceeding this figure.

Where a heavy partition, such as concrete blockwork, is built on a timber floor it may be sufficient to place two floor joists together if the partition runs parallel with the joists. If it runs across the joists it may

Joist size mm	Joist size in.	Joist spacing 400 mm (16 in)	450 mm (18 in)
38 x 75	(1½ x 3)	1.03 m (3 ft 3 in)	0.93 m (3 ft)
38 x 100	(1½ x 4)	1.74 m (5 ft 6 in)	1.57 (5 ft 2 in)
38 x 125	(1½ x 5)	2.50 (8 ft 2 in)	2.31 (7 ft 6 in)
38 x 150	(1½ x 6)	2.99 (9 ft 9 in)	2.83 (9 ft 2 in)
38 x 175	(1½ x 7)	3.48 11 ft 5 in	3.29 (10 ft 9 in)
38 x 200	(1½ x 8)	3.96 (12 ft 9 in)	3.75 (12 ft 1 in)
38 x 225	(1½ x 9)	4.44 (14 ft 3 in)	4.20 (13 ft 9 in)

be necessary to use joists of greater size than the foregoing table.

Furniture counts as live load and normally no extra joist strength is required.

In the case of old cottages it is advisable to check the condition and sizes of floor joists as they may not be of adequate strength or have been weakened by settlement or decay.

Ceiling joists

Ceiling joists under a pitched roof are usually a structural part of the roof as they serve as ties secured to the rafters and wall plates at the ends. They prevent the thrust of the rafters spreading the roof or exerting outward thrust on the walls.

The Building Regulations give tables for the various spans and for ceiling joists of 38 mm (3 in), 44 mm (1¾ in) and 50 mm (2 in) thickness and depths ranging in similar sizes to those mentioned for floor joists. Where there is no floor load to be carried, ceiling joists for small houses are usually either 38 mm (1½ in) x 75 mm (3 in) or x 100 mm (4 in). In some cases the 44 mm (1¾ in) thickness is preferred and in fewer cases the 50 mm (2 in).

The Building Regulations give tabulated data for all sizes but the data given here is for the most economical thickness—38 mm (1½ in).

Ceiling Joist size mm	Joist size in.	Joist spacing 400 mm (16 in)	450 mm (18 in)	
38 x 75	(1½ x 3)	1.8 m (6 ft)	1.74 m (5 ft 7 in)	
38 x 100	(1½ x 4)	2.39 m (7 ft 9 in)	2.31 m (7 ft 7 in)	
38 x 125	(1½ x 5)	2.98 m (9 ft 7 in)	2.87 m (9 ft 3 in)	Maximum span of joists
38 x 150	(1½ x 6)	3.57 m (11 ft 6 in)	3.44 m (11 ft 2 in)	
38 x 175	(1½ x 7)	4.14 m (13 ft 6 in)	4.00 m (13 ft)	
38 x 200	(1½ x 8)	4.72 m (15 ft 5 in)	4.55 m (14 ft 9 in)	

The span across the full width of a house or bungalow roof is not necessarily the span of the ceiling joists as specified in the table. If intermediate support is provided on interior load-bearing walls or on strong timbers called binders, (which are placed over the joists at right angles to them and nailed from below), the tabular span is taken between the points of support. For example if a room is 3.7 m (12 ft) wide between outer and inner loadbearing walls, and a binder is placed mid-way between the two, the tabular span can be taken as 1.8 m (6 ft). From the table, ceiling joists 38 mm (1½ in) x 75 mm (3 in) spaced at 400 mm (16 in) centres are suitable.

An alternative to placing binders above the ceiling joists is to place a beam below. This may be of timber, steel or reinforced concrete.

Chapter 6
Roofing and roof construction

Pitched roofs may be of any angle over two degrees to the horizontal. The pitch must be suitable for the type of roof covering to ensure weathertightness. Below ten degrees of roof is regarded as flat, though a slope is necessary for drainage.

Tiled roofs

Most house roofs are now covered with tiles of pre-cast concrete with a coloured surface. Clay tiles and natural slates are still used to a less extent but are more costly.

Pre-cast concrete tiles are made in a wide range of shapes and sizes, from traditional plain tiles, 265 mm x 165 mm (10½ in x 6½ in) to the largest tiles which are approximately 430 mm x 380 mm (17 in x 15 in). All patterns are illustrated in manufacturers catalogues which can be seen at any builders merchants.

Plain tiles have a double end lap and are hung to battens by the projecting nibs at the rear head.

Single-lap tiles include traditional profiles, such as pantiles and Roman tiles, but with interlocking side laps which form positive weather stops. Pantiles have a roll-and-trough cross section. Roman tiles have a double roll separate by a flat section. Both produce interesting shadow lines. The largest tiles are flat and some resemble large slates.

Ridge and hip tiles and valley tiles are made. Alternatively, valleys can be lined with sheet lead.

Most modern tiles are of the single lap type, including the pantile profile. The head lap is adjustable but as the side edges interlock this lap is fixed.

The minimum recommended roof pitch for most single lap tiles is 30 degrees, with reinforced underfelt draped over the rafters and tiling battens nailed over the underfelt. If the rafters are boarded or covered with insulating sheeting, and underfelt on top with tiling battens on counter-battens, the pitch may be lower.

Plain tiles should have a roof pitch of not less than 35 degrees, with reinforced underfelt. In a position exposed to very strong gales 40 degrees or more is recommended.

There are several patterns of large pre-cast concrete tiles which are suitable for very low pitches — 17½ degrees down to 12½ degrees, with underfelt. The manufacturers' recommendations should be followed for pitch and other details.

Roof construction

There are two types of pitched roof construction. The traditional method, still used, is to build it up on the site with rafters, ridges, purlins and ties — the latter serving also as ceiling joists. A modern method, which is increasingly used, is to obtain prefabricated trussed rafters which can be quickly erected — of these, more later.

A timber pitched roof consists of sloping rafters cut at the lower end to fit over horizontal wall plates and at the top bevelled against a ridge board.

For small span roofs, i.e. a lean-to, a centre ridge with a collar (see diagram) are suitable.

With the ceiling joists the pitched roof

50

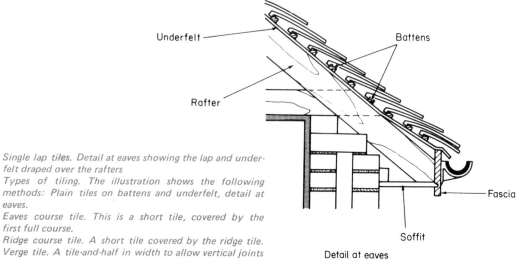

Underfelt

Battens

Rafter

Fascia

Soffit

Single lap tiles. Detail at eaves showing the lap and under-felt draped over the rafters
Types of tiling. The illustration shows the following methods: Plain tiles on battens and underfelt, detail at eaves.
Eaves course tile. This is a short tile, covered by the first full course.
Ridge course tile. A short tile covered by the ridge tile.
Verge tile. A tile-and-half in width to allow vertical joints to be staggered

Detail at eaves

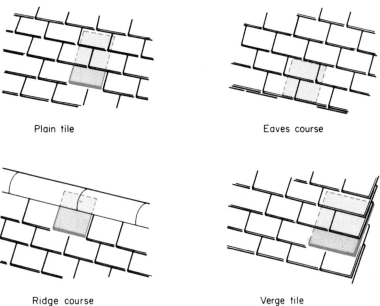

Plain tile

Eaves course

Ridge course

Verge tile

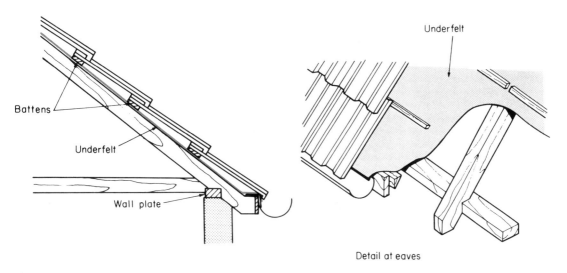

Battens

Underfelt

Wall plate

Underfelt

Detail at eaves

Pitched roofs of small spans. The collar and the tie strengthen the roof frames and prevent the rafters thrusting the walls outwards

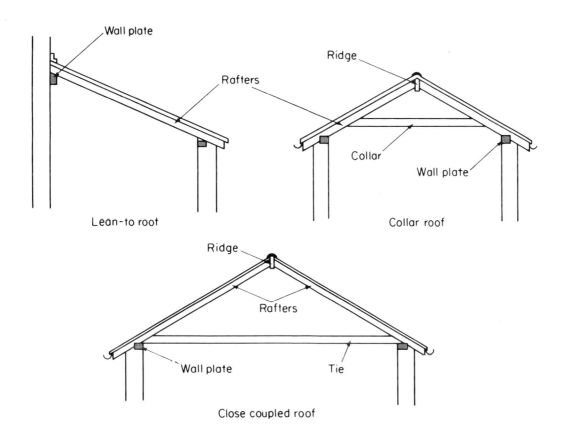

Wall plate

Rafters

Lean-to roof

Ridge

Rafters

Collar

Wall plate

Collar roof

Ridge

Rafters

Wall plate

Tie

Close coupled roof

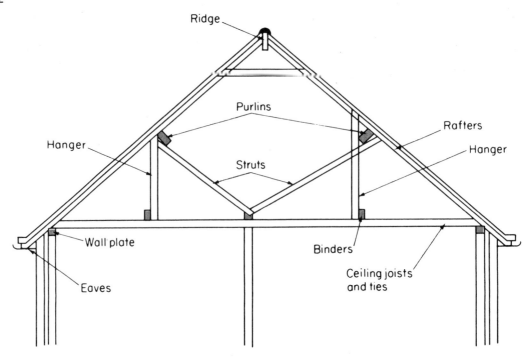

Ridge

Purlins

Rafters

Hanger

Hanger

Struts

Wall plate

Binders

Eaves

Ceiling joists
and ties

forms a triangle — a strong form of frame. Intermediate support to the rafters may be given by fixing purlins, which are placed under and at right angles to the rafters and are usually supported at the ends on walls with intermediate support on struts resting on partition walls.

The ceiling joists or ties may be nailed at wall plate level to form a flat ceiling across the full span of the roof. Alternatively they may be raised some distance above the wall plates and nailed to the sides of the rafters so that they give extra head room.

A pitched roof may have gable ends or hipped ends. The gable roof is the simpler as the common rafters are all of equal length, given an equal span. The purlin ends can be built into the gable walls.

A hipped roof is more complicated as a series of shortened rafters, called jack rafters, must be cut to a double bevel against the hip rafters. The hip rafters

Traditional framed roof. Rafters with intermediate support on purlins and struts. The hangers and binders give intermediate support to the ceiling joist

must be cut to fit over the wall plates and against the ridge end. Purlins must be supported on struts of trusses.

Where a loft room is placed within a roof, windows may be arranged in the gable ends. Windows can also be placed in the roof, as illustrated. This is, of course essential with a hipped roof. The rafters must be trimmed to form a suitable opening either for a dormer window or a rooflight.

Rafter sizes

The size of the rafters depends upon the pitch of the roof and the span between points of support. A table of sizes is given in the Building Regulations for rafters having a pitch of more than 10 degrees but not more than 22½ degrees. Another

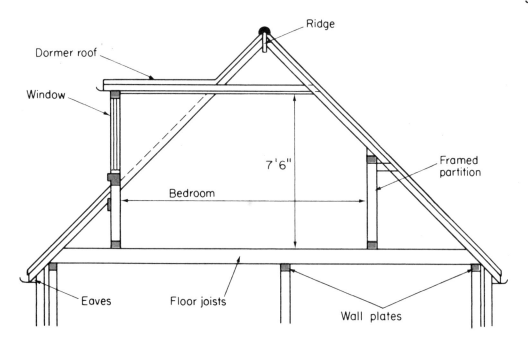

Ridge

Dormer roof

Window

7'6"

Framed partition

Bedroom

Eaves Floor joists

Wall plates

Roof room and dormer. The dormer extends the area of headroom as well as providing a window. The side frames are supported on the floor joists

table is for a pitch more than 22½ degrees but not more than 30 degrees. A third for pitches between 30 degrees and 42½ degrees.

The rafters should be normally spaced at 400 mm (16 in) or 450 mm (18 in), whichever spacing is adopted for the ceiling joists. This is so that the rafters can be nailed alongside the ceiling joists.

The lower the pitch, the deeper the dimension of the rafters, as the bending stresses are greater than at high pitches. For example, for pitches of 22½ degrees and lower the maximum span for 38 mm x 100 mm (1½ in x 4 in) rafters spaced at 400 mm (16 in) centres is 2.39 m (7 ft 8 in) but for pitches between 30 degrees and 42½ degrees for this size rafters the maximum span is 2.81 m (9 ft 2 in). These figures are for tiles of normal light weights. The Building Regulations provide data for all pitches and weights.

Prefabricated timber trussed rafters are

manufactured for erection on site at 600 mm (2 ft) centres, as illustrated.

Pitched roofs for covering with corrugated sheets of asbestos-cement, aluminium alloy, galvanised steel or plastic, can be of low pitch — not less than 10 degrees. The manufacturer's instructions should be followed regarding the necessary supporting timbers for these sheets as sizes and strengths vary with the pattern and material.

The construction of timber roofs for sheeting is different from that described for tiles. Horizontal purlins are fixed parallel to the wall plates and ridge, spaced so that they support the head and tail of the sheets where they overlap and also with intermediate support for the longer sheets. The purlins must be supported at the ends and, if necessary at intermediate positions.

Fixing corrugated and plastic sheeting

Purlin joined to beam with a metal framing anchor. These anchors are fixed with special nails provided

Driving screws, galvanised, with plastic cup washers should be used for fixing corrugated sheets. Holes should be drilled in the sheets, not punched. Suitable fixings can be obtained when buying the sheets. For an example of a structure with a roof covered with corrugated translucent plastic sheeting see page 87.

The laps of translucent plastic sheeting should be sealed with sealing tape to prevent dust and fine debris accumulating within the lap.

Corrugated sheeting tends to collect condensed moisture on the underside in a damp cold atmosphere. Sheeting of asbestos-cement or of metal can be insulated underneath by first covering the roof structure with insulation board. This will also reduce heat loss in winter and excessive solar heating in summer.

Flat roofs

A flat roof is any roof from level up to 10 degrees slope. For draining rainwater a fall of not less than 38 mm (1½ in) in 3 m (10 ft) is necessary. Where the roof is for access only for maintenance or repair, and for boarding and covering with bituminous felt, the timber joists of structural grade softwoods, spaced at 400 mm (16 in) or at 450 mm (18 in) centres should be of the sizes specified for ceiling joists (page 47).

If a flat roof is to be used as a balcony or sun roof stronger joists are required. The sizes specified for floor joists (see page 45) may be suitable with a slight reduction in the span.

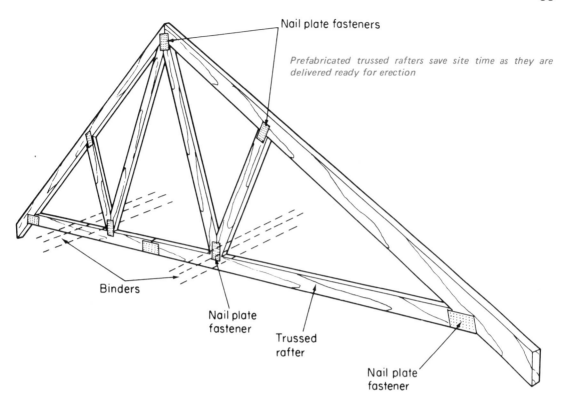

Nail plate fasteners

Prefabricated trussed rafters save site time as they are delivered ready for erection

Binders

Nail plate fastener

Trussed rafter

Nail plate fastener

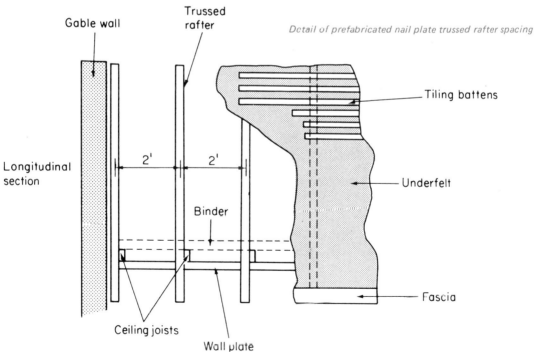

Gable wall

Trussed rafter

Detail of prefabricated nail plate trussed rafter spacing

Tiling battens

Underfelt

Longitudinal section

2'

2'

Binder

Fascia

Ceiling joists

Wall plate

Prefabricated trussed rafters

56

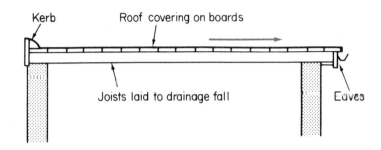

Kerb · Roof covering on boards · Joists laid to drainage fall · Eaves

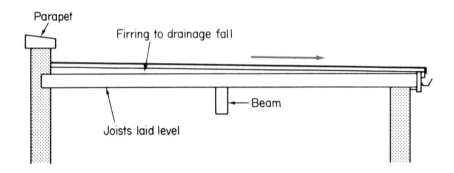

Parapet · Firring to drainage fall · Beam · Joists laid level

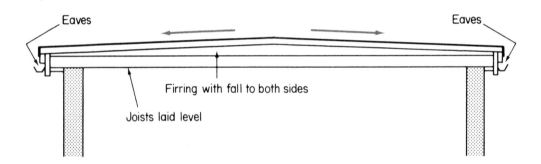

Eaves · Eaves · Firring with fall to both sides · Joists laid level

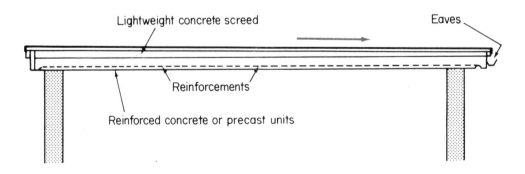

Lightweight concrete screed · Eaves · Reinforcements · Reinforced concrete or precast units

Flat roofs, but with a slight fall for drainage. Thermal insulation should be added for dwellings. A concrete flat roof needs temperary shuttering or pre-cast concrete beam units

Garden shed roofs are usually of light construction. In some cases, however they may be too light with consequent sagging. Snow and wind loads must be considered and it is advisable to comply with the table on page 38 even for light sheds. The exception is that for spans not exceeding 1.5 m (5 ft) 38 mm x 50 mm (1½ in x 2 in), joists are suitable.

The fall for drainage may be obtained by fixing the roof joists at the required slope but, for a level ceiling, the joists should be fixed level and tapered firring pieces nailed on top. Most timber suppliers will cut these firrings to order — machine sawing two tapered pieces out of one length of timber.

If on brick or block walls, flat roof joists should be securely nailed to the wall plate timbers. The wall plates should be fixed to the wall top with anchor bolts. Failure to fix securely may result in the roof being lifted by wind suction in a gale.

Corrugated asbestos-cement sheets and translucent plastic sheets are sometimes used on flat roofs. These are not very satisfactory at very low pitches. If they are so used it should be noted that they will not support any extra load and you should not stand or kneel on them. Accidents have been caused by standing on asbestos-cement roofs. Where access for repairs is necessary, scaffold boards should be placed and secured over the roof sheets.

Chapter 7
Joinery-tools, materials, joints

Joinery differs from carpentry as it calls for planed and well finished surfaces, accurate dimensions and preparation of joints. So, in addition to the tools used in carpentry (see page 43), further tools are needed. There are numerous joinery tools but the following is a basic collection which will serve for most home joinery, including simple built-ins and furniture.

Tools

Tools must be kept in good condition if satisfactory work is to be done. Plane and chisel blades must be frequently sharpened. Saws must be re-set and sharpened as the teeth wear (most tool shops will undertake this rather tricky job). All tools must be protected from damp.

Benches

A bench is essential but it need not be an elaborate or expensive one. You can knock up a useful bench using softwood, at least 50 mm x 50 mm (2 in x 2 in) for the legs and 20 mm x 150 mm (¾ in x 3 in) for the rails. Fix rails all round the top and also about half way down the legs by nailing or screwing. The top should be covered with planed boards about 20 mm (¾ in) thick nailed or screwed to the rails. Punch the nail heads down, using oval wire nails, and countersink screw heads slightly below the surface.

A woodworker's vice (of moderate size) should be fixed to one side of the bench. A quick release mechanism is useful but not essential. Line the cheeks with pieces of 12 mm (½ in) planed wood. For light jobs, a portable vice, which is simply clamped to the bench or even a kitchen table, is sufficient.

Planes and saws

You will need a general, purpose plane, preferably of steel, at least 230 mm (9 in). A grooving or fillister plane is necessary if you want to make built-ins or furniture. This enables rebates and grooves to be made for doors, frames and jointing.

A general purpose, 600 mm (24 in) saw, medium teeth, and a tenon saw for fine cutting are sufficient for most jobs, but a hacksaw or frame saw is useful for a variety of small jobs. A coping saw is similar but has a fine blade and the frame shape allows curves to be cut in boards or plywood.

A spokeshave is useful for rounding off ends of small sections of wood. A shaper plane or tool with serrated blades which are interchangeable (there are several proprietary makes), is useful for various shaping jobs.

Electric tools

A portable electric drill saves time and labour if you have much drilling to do. There are various accessories, such as circular saws and drill stands, which can be fitted to it.

If you want to make much joinery — for example, and furniture — an electric woodworking machine in your workshop will enable sawing, drilling, turning, planing, rebating, grooving, sanding and most jointing jobs to be done speedily. But a good universal machine costs a few hundred pounds and is hardly justified for occasional woodworking.

Small hand tools

In addition to the large claw hammer, mentioned under carpentry, a smaller Warrington hammer for driving small nails and panel pins is essential.

A gimlet for boring small holes, a bradawl for smaller hole, and a brace and set of bits will serve for most drilling jobs. A geared hand drill with a set of twist drills is more convenient than a brace for some jobs. For drilling holes in walls for wall-plugs a masonry drill is necessary.

A try square and a marking gauge are necessary for setting out joints and lengths. A 600 mm (24 in) folding rule and a flexible steel rule 1.8 in (6 ft) long will be useful for measuring.

You will need screwdrivers, small and large, or a ratchet type with a set of driver bits and small diameter drill bits. This should include a star driver for fixing screws with star shaped 'Posidriv' slots. Pincers are required for removing nails.

Chisels, narrow, medium and up to 25 mm (1 in) for cutting. Use gouge chisels if you want to cut concave grooves. If you are going in for wood carving buy a good set of wood carving tools — these have various shapes and are better adapted than ordinary chisels for the purpose.

Scrapers are required for removing paint and varnish; but it is advisable to apply a paint removing paste on thick finishes to soften them. A blowlamp or blowtorch is an alternative but take care if working on delicate woods—the flame can mark them. The blowtorch is more convenient than a blowlamp and is finding increasing favour with the d.i.y. enthusiast.

Finally, you will need a carborundum stone and an oil can. You can hone chisels and plane blades accurately if you use a honing gauge which holds the blade at the correct angle.

Materials

Timbers are divided into softwoods and hardwoods but the densities in both classes vary and in this matter the terms are misleading. Softwoods come from the conifer group — fir, pines, redwood, spruce, red cedar, larch and hemlock. Hardwoods come from the broad-leaf trees — including oak, mahogany, teak and many African, and Asian timbers now widely used, including abura, afara, African walnut, iroko, makore, obeche, sapele, utile, and padauk.

Softwoods are used for standard mass produced joinery including window and door frames, floorboards, built-ins and porches, for paint or preservative strain finishes.

Parana pine is a superior softwood which is recommended for good quality joinery and furniture. It is close grained and works well. For interior work it looks attractive if finished with a transparent sealer or varnish.

Wood with large or loose knots is not good for general joinery but knotty pine boards look attractive on walls and ceilings and for cottage type built-ins.

Hardwoods are generally denser and more costly than softwoods. In most cases the appearance is good and the surface is merely sealed. Densities and working qualities vary. Teak and iroko, for example, are very hard. Mahogany varies but Honduras mahogony works and finishes well.

Plywoods and blockboards

The thinner plywoods are three-ply and one face is usually superior in appearance than the other. The core is at right angles to the face veneers. Multiply has a core of two, three or more plies.

Standard plywood thicknesses are

mm	in
3.2	1/8
5.0	3/16
6.5	1/4
9.5	3/8
12.5	1/2
16.0	5/8
19.0	3/4

Blockboard is made with blocks up to 25 mm (1 in) wide as the core with facing veneers. Some types have decorative veneer or hardwood, on ply backing.

Laminboard has a core of narrow strips of wood, faced with veneer, as with blockboard, on ply backing.

Standard thicknesses are

mm	in
12.5	1/2
16.0	5/8
19.0	3/4
22.0	7/8

Composite boards

These are plywoods faced with plastics or with sheet metal and are made under proprietary names.

Composite boards with cores of insulating material faced with plywood are available for use as thermal insulating partitions or linings.

There are several grades of plywood, blockboard and laminboard according to the quality of the veneers.

Ordinary plywoods are made with water soluble adhesives and are only suitable for interior use in normal dry conditions. Exterior grade plywoods are made with synthetic resin adhesives which have high resistance to damp and superior strength.

Chipboard or particle boards

This may be either boards or panels made of wood chips processed with synthetic resin binder and compressed. There are several types but the most widely used are of medium density.

These boards or panels are free from warping and can be used for large jointless surfaces such as wardrobes, cupboard doors and table tops

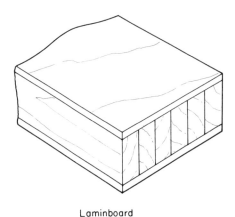

Laminboard

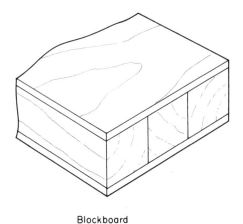

Blockboard

The boards do not warp under normal conditions and cost less than natural wood. They can be used for built-ins, partitions, and there are proprietary types with special surfaces and veneers. For shelves and making furniture, the boards are obtainable in a range of widths and lengths with the edges also veneered.

A special grade of chipboard, 19 mm (¾ in), is made for flooring panels. Ordinary chipboards are not suitable for exterior damp conditions but a special damp-resisting type is made. All types are easily sawn and can be fixed by nailing or screwing.

Hardboards

Dense boards of wood fibre are called hardboards. Ordinary hardboards are generally used for such work as backing cupboards but with suitable framing can be used for many purposes, including built-ins.

Tempered hardboard is a superior grade of high damp resistance and strength, and is intended mainly for exterior use. For outside use, however, it needs protecting with paint.

It can be used to form a new floor surface over an existing boarded floor. Ordinary hardboard is suitable for this purpose if the floor is to be covered with wall-to-wall carpet, vinyl, or for cork or other flooring tiles.

Decorated hardboards have a variety of special finishes — enamelled or lacquered; plastic faced; printed wood grain effects with a plastic finish; and veneered with natural wood.

Perforated and slotted hardboards are used for ventilation panels, decorative effects and to provide wall panels with demountable hooks for hanging tools, clips and pictures.

Insulating boards

Low density fibreboards are in this class, in thicknesses of 12 mm (½ in), 18 mm (¾ in) and 25 mm (1 in). They are suitable for lining walls partitions and ceilings, but generally the fire retardant grade should be used where the surface of the board is exposed.

The thermal insulation of walls and partitions can be improved by lining with insulation board on wood battens spaced 400 mm (16 in) centres. The boards can also be nailed to ceiling joists. Wood boarded floors on open joists can be insulated by laying insulation board between the joists and the floor boards. Timber flat roofs can be insulated in the same way and concrete flat roofs may have bitumen impregnated insulation board bedded in bitumen on the concrete.

Laminated plastic sheets, 1.5 mm thick, which have a dense non-absorbent surface, are made in a wide range of colours and decorative patterns. They must be stuck to a rigid base, such as blockboard, with an impact adhesive.

Plasterboard is an excellent material for lining partitions, walls and ceilings.

For thermal insulation foil-backed plasterboard should be used, as the bright aluminium backing reflects heat rays. But the backing must face an air space, so this type of board must be nailed either to timber frames or battens.

Weather boards

Wood boards for external cladding may be of a good quality softwood (preferably impregnated by the timber supplier with preservative), or of Western red cedar which has high resistance to decay, or a suitable hardwood.

Horizontal boarding should have rebated (overlapping) edges. The 'shiplap' pattern is generally favoured as it has an attractive curved upper edge.

Vertical boarding should be grooved and tongued with a chamfered vee or curved edge. Some wide boards are made which are moulded to appear as two or three boards of varying width.

Weather boards should be nailed, with galvanised steel or aluminum oval or lost head nails, to supporting battens or timber framing, spaced not more than 450 mm (18 in) centres. They should not be tightly cramped at the joints but allow freedom of swelling and shrinkage, which is inevitable even with painted boards. If tightly cramped they will corrugate when swollen by damp absorption. The edge joint should be barely a touch fit. In very dry weather a slight clearance should be left at the edges.

Softwood weather boards may be finished by oil painting—primer, under-coat and gloss coat (two gloss coats are better than one to start with). Alternatively, a preservative stain finish may be applied. But this should be renewed every three years.

Hardwood boards may be sealed with a polyurethane sealer or a high quality transparent varnish. But these, too, need renewal at intervals of a few years. To do this, first scrape and rub down with sandpaper to remove the old finish, and then apply two coats of the new finish.

Care should be taken to seal the ends of weather boards, with paint or sealer, as damp is readily drawn through the end grain. This is where rot usually starts.

Generally, horizontal weather boarding is better than vertical as rainwater is less likely to enter the joints. It is easier to remove a horizontal defective board and replace with new.

Joints

Joints can be cut with a tenon saw or, if dowelled, with a drill. They may be glued, nailed or screwed together. Some of the most useful and simple joints are illustrated.

Boarding for external and internal use. These boards can be used for cladding sheds, workshops and garden buildings or for interior decorative use on walls and ceilings

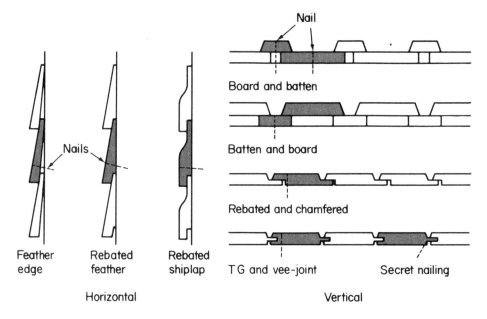

Feather edge · Rebated feather · Rebated shiplap

Horizontal

Nail · Board and batten · Batten and board · Rebated and chamfered · T G and vee-joint · Secret nailing

Vertical

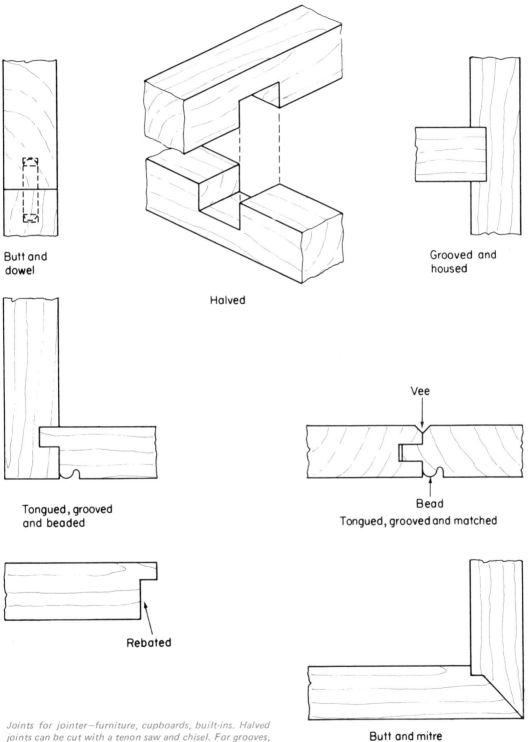

Butt and
dowel

Halved

Grooved and
housed

Tongued, grooved
and beaded

Vee

Bead

Tongued, grooved and matched

Rebated

Butt and mitre

*Joints for jointer—furniture, cupboards, built-ins. Halved
joints can be cut with a tenon saw and chisel. For grooves,
a grooving plane is preferable*

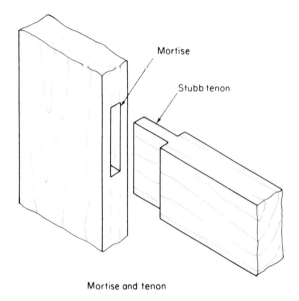

Mortise

Stubb tenon

Mortise and tenon

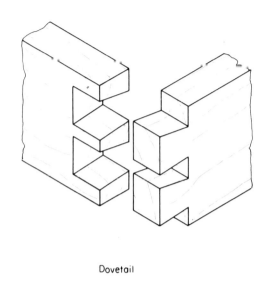

Dovetail

A butt joint can be secured by two or three wood dowels glued in. The holes drilled in each piece of wood must correspond exactly. For this purpose a dowelling jig should be used.

A halved (half lap) joint is simple to form by making two saw cuts at the end of each piece of wood, for a corner joint, or two saw cuts and then cutting the waste out with a chisel for a cross halved joint.

A simple corner joint for rails is the rabbet (rebated joint), with the end of one piece rebated to allow the plain end of the other piece to be glued into it.

A grooved joint is formed by cutting a groove across the grain of one piece so that the plain end of the other piece can be glued into it. A good simple joint for joining a shelf to a side support. To conceal the joint the groove can be stopped about 18 mm (¾ in) short of the front edge though this needs extra care in chiselling.

A dovetail joint makes a strong fixing but needs careful setting out and exact cutting. There are several forms of this.

A mitre joint for a corner consists of the ends of both pieces bevelled at 45 degrees.

A mortise slot can be cut by drilling and chiselling. The tenon cut with a tenon saw, also used for cutting dovetails. Electric woodworking appliances simplify this sort of work

It has no strength in itself but can be made secure by glueing a triangular corner block into the corner.

Multiple dovetailed joists, as used in making drawers, are for the skilled and patient woodworker. The combed joint is similar except that the joint projections and recesses are not of dovetail shape. These joints are easier to make if a machine saw with a special attachment is used.

Mortise and tenon joints are used chiefly for joining rails to stiles (horizontals to verticals) in panelled doors. They are cut by drilling and chiselling to remove the waste for the mortise recess and by cutting with the tenon saw to form the tenon.

Another type of mortise and tenon is for joining corners of frames for built-ins and furniture. This is a tenon at the end of one piece fitted into an open slot in the other piece.

Joint fittings

In many cases cut joints can be avoided by using proprietary fittings or devices of metal or nylon plastic. A very useful type consists of a pair of blocks, with holes for screwing to the inside corner of a frame, such as the rails of a cupboard, with integral dowel projections on one block which engage with corresponding holes in the other. This has the advantage of being easily demountable.

Steel corner brackets for screw fixing can be used for supporting shelves and for securing an internal corner in a frame.

Chapter 8
Windows, doors and staircases

Windows and doors come in a variety of types and sizes and all are described in this chapter. Patio doors (or french windows) are also covered. Unless you are building a house or reconstructing a very old one, you will probably never need to construct a staircase. However, a few notes on staircases are given at the end of this chapter.

Types of window

Windows are made in a range of standard sizes, suitable for houses and bungalows, but there are special types which can be made to order.

The four materials used for windows are:

1. *Wood.* Softwood for painting; hardwood for sealing or varnishing.

2. *Steel.* Galvanised, for painting.

3. *Aluminium alloy.* Usually fitted in a hardwood surround. No painting needed.

4. *Plastics* in extruded sections.

Wood casement windows

Mass produced wood casement windows, manufactured by members of the British Woodwork Manufacturers Association under their EJMA mark, are good low-cost windows. It is essential to keep them well protected by painting, especially by good initial painting when they are clean and dry. They can be obtained ready treated with a preservative which will take a paint finish. The various types of casement windows are as follows.

Casements, side hung (some with top hung vents), traditional in design, single frames 438 mm (1 ft 5¼ in) wide and multiple frames with two, three and four lights divided by mullions. These come in types, plain lights for single panes of glass and divided lights with glazing bars for small panes.

Casements, landscape or sunshine types, with a fixed single wide pane and some with side hung openable casements, others with top hung openable vent lights.

Casements, pivot range. These have square shaped panes, with centre pivoted casements and single, double or treble frames. Pivot windows are reversible—which is a considerable advantage for cleaning especially upstairs windows—and with suitable fittings they can be set open in any position.

Feature windows are based on the landscape or sunshine large pane windows. The jambs are extended from floor level with a middle rail which forms a panel below for glazing or filling with boarding or exterior grade plywood. Some types are made in combination with a door frame, one type for inward opening door, another for outward opening.

A typical section through a casement window, as fixed in a cavity wall, is shown.

Sash windows

Sash windows, double hung for vertical sliding, of traditional appearance, but with spring balance fittings, in place of the old sash cords and balance weights, are made for plain panes or with glazing bars for small panes.

Sash windows are associated architecturally with Georgian houses.

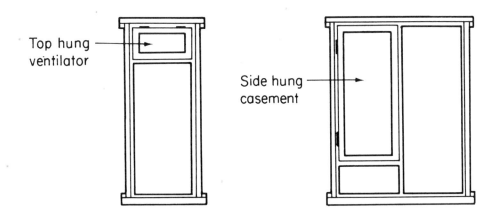

Top hung ventilator

Side hung casement

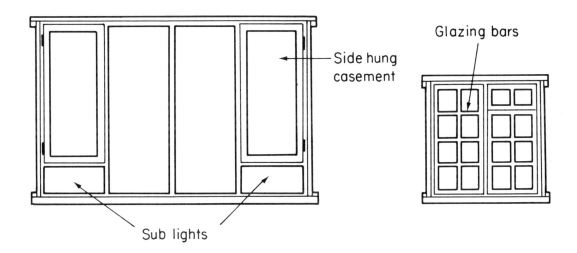

Side hung casement

Glazing bars

Sub lights

Standard wood casement windows

These are some of the many standard windows available in a wide range of sizes. They can be treated with a special preservative which can be painted over

Bow windows

Bow windows, with glazing bars for small panes, are also made in several standard sizes and these, too, are suitable for Georgian style houses.

A moulded glass fibre roof and fascia is supplied as an extra by the makers. This makes installation easier, but a flat boarded roof, lead covered, can be built on the bow frame if preferred.

Bay windows

There are four standard plan shapes of bay windows. Square bays have returns at 90 degrees; splayed bays have returns at 30–45 and 60 degrees; curved bays are of two radii — 1.6 m (5 ft 2 in) and 3.7 m (12 ft 2 in) — the former with a bold projection, the latter with a shallow projection.

Square and splayed bays are also made with a single return, right hand or left hand, for fitting into a wall corner.

68

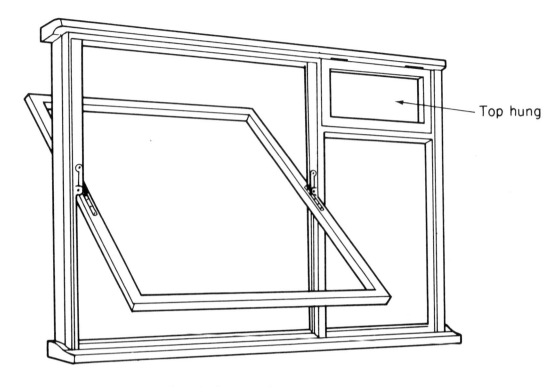

Top hung

Wood pivoted windows

Standard windows with wide panes give a better view. The pivot type is convenient as it can be reversed for cleaning

Fixed

Fixed

Standard wood landscape windows

Plastics windows

Rigid PVC extruded sections are used for making window frames by several well-known manufactures. These originated on the Continent and this is sometimes evident from some of the styles which are available.

The weathering and other characteristics appear to be satisfactory. They are fitted with clip-on glazing beads.

PVC plastics are also used by some manufacturers as a sheathing over a wood or metal core which is thus protected from damp and needs no painting.

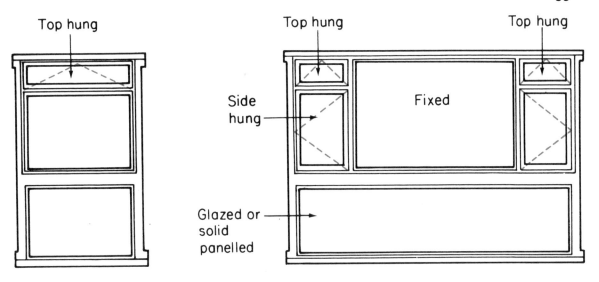

Feature windows

Feature windows have the sill at floor level. The combined window/door frame is convenient for a narrow hall

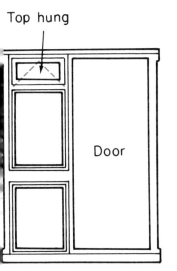

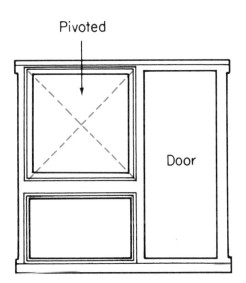

Combined window/door frame

Steel windows

These windows are made of steel sections with hinged casements fitting into a fixed frame. The wide range of sizes and types approximate to the range for standard wood windows. The windows are galvanised which protects against corrosion, provided the galvanised is not damaged by rough usage. Painting on the galvanised surface gives additional protection. Side hung, top hung and pivot casements are available.

Steel windows should be set in a wood surround which gives a better appearance and also protects the steel frame during transport and fixing.

Aluminium windows

Aluminium alloy in extruded sections is used for many types of windows and there are several proprietary ranges and types. The lighter sections are suitable for domestic

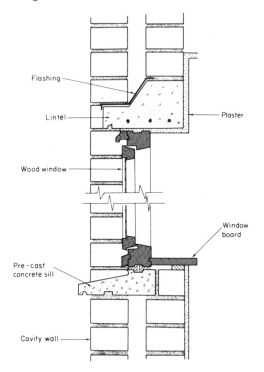

use. Most aluminium windows are horizontal sliding fitted with nylon draught stripping.

In addition to the normal ranges, some manufacturers offer an interior range for fixing inside existing windows to form a double window for thermal insulation and draught proofing. Most are easy to fix with simple tools. The glass is usually fixed in plastic channels, and no putty is required.

For the exterior windows, the metal frame should be set in a hardwood surround which protects the window against damage in handling and adds to the appearance.

Aluminium windows do not corrode in normal atmospheres where atmospheric pollution is low. The surface needs only occasional cleaning with soapy water. Anodised transparent finish gives a slightly better appearance but is not necessary for protection. Some manufacturers offer acrylic plastic finishes in various colours.

If you wish to paint aluminium frames a zinc chromate primer should be used. Ordinary lead based primer does not take well.

Left, detail of a standard wood window set in a cavity wall. Other types of lintel and sill are optional

Balanced sash windows are suitable for Georgian style houses. Modern standard types are usually spring balanced

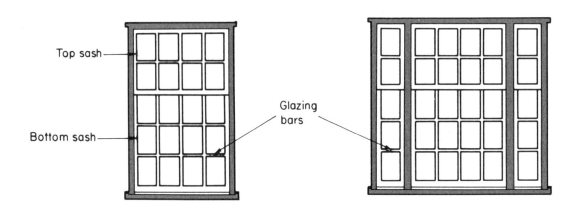

Glazing

Clear sheet glass, as normally used for house windows, has blemishes which slightly distort vision. The 3 mm thickness (24 oz per sq. ft.) is used for small to moderate size panes and the 4 mm (32 oz per sq. ft) for larger panes not exceeding 2 m x 1.25 m (6 ft 6 in x 4 ft).

Float glass is now widely used in place of sheet, as the surfaces are perfectly flat and give undistorted vision. The 3 mm thickness up to 1.27 m x 1.27 m (4 ft x 4 ft) panes and the 5 mm up to 2.5 m x 2.25 m (8 ft x 7 ft) for positions of normal

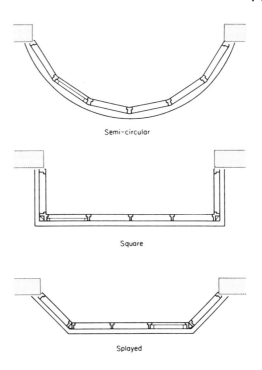

Semi-circular

Square

Splayed

Right, standard bay windows are made in a range of widths and projections. They add floor are and extend the view

Galvanised steel windows of a variety of types and sizes are made. They look better set in a wood surround

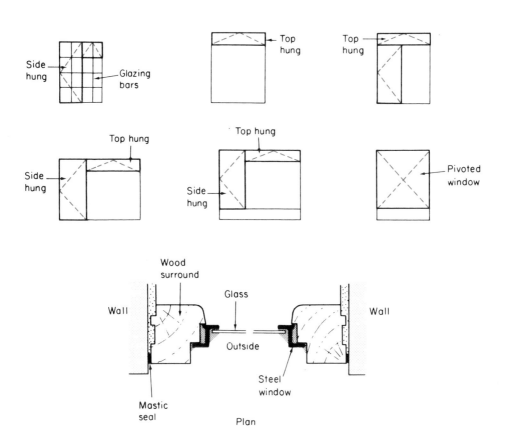

Side hung / Glazing bars / Top hung / Top hung

Side hung / Top hung / Top hung / Side hung / Pivoted window

Wood surround / Glass / Wall / Wall / Outside / Steel window / Mastic seal / Plan

exposure. Greater thicknesses are made for larger areas. These are used mainly for shop windows in place of the more costly plate glass

Solar control glass, tinted bronze or green for reducing solar energy in hot weather, is useful in large glass areas, particularly south facing. Rolled translucent glass with a pattern on one side, flat on the other, used where vision obscuration is required.

Wired glass, with wire mesh embedded, is used where fire resistance is required. The transparent wired (Georgian) glass gives clear vision and the translucent wired cast glass obscured vision.

Glazing methods

Linseed oil putty is the traditional glazing material for wood windows. It is not suitable for metal windows, for which a special metal glazing putty is available. There are also proprietary multi-purpose putty materials for use with wood or metal frames.

Linseed oil putty should not be painted until it has started to harden, which generally means waiting about a fortnight. But it should be painted before it dries out; otherwise it will crack.

Before placing the glass in position the rebate into which it fits should be back puttied, applying the putty with thumb and finger. Smooth it slightly with the putty knife, then place the glass and press it gently all round. A few steel glazing sprigs should be tapped in each side, top and bottom to secure the glass. Puttying should then be completed with the knife (or a small trowel). The edges should be trimmed straight and the excess putty squeezed out at the back of the rebate cut straight and flush.

Double glazing

There are two types of double glazing. First, the fixing of a second pane of glass to an existing single glazed frame. Second, the sealed glazing unit (or insulating glass) which is manufactured by separating two sheets of glass to form an air gap and sealing the edges.

Most new windows for double glazing are fitted with insulating glass in a rebate deeper than is normal for single glazing. One type of insulating unit is made with the inside and outside glasses fused together at the edge to form a single unit. Two thicknesses are made, with air gap of 5 mm and 7 mm. The depth of the rebate should be not less than 11 mm for the 5 mm air space units and 13 mm for the 7 mm air space type. The units are made in standard sizes to fit modern standard frames. The manufacturers of double glazing units supply printed fixing instructions which should be carefully followed.

Sealed double glazing units have the air gap dehydrated in manufacture so that internal condensation (within the air gap) should not occur.

Double glazing by fixing a second sheet of glass in a light plastic or metal frame to an existing single glazed window reduces the tendency to condensation of moisture from the room atmosphere but cannot completely prevent it. If this form of double glazing is in a hinged or horizontal sliding frame it is an easy matter to open it and wipe off any condensed moisture.

Sound resistant double glazing must have an air space of not less than 100 mm (4 in) to be effective. The two sheets of glass must be fixed in a double frame, or a deep frame with inner and outer rebates. Special double casement windows are made for this purpose.

Doors

Doors for houses may be of wood, metal, or plastic.

Wood doors are of three distinct types; flush doors consisting of a wood core faced both sides either with plywood or hardboard; panelled doors consisting of framed vertical stiles and horizontal rails grooved to accommodate panels, and ledged boarded doors.

All types are made in softwood and hardwood; the latter are more costly though of superior quality. Softwood doors are for painting, whilst hardwood doors are for finishing with polish or a sealing varnish to enhance the natural colour and grain and also to provide an easily cleaned surface.

Fire resisting doors are made to comply with the Building Regulations for use where a house garage has a communicating door with the hall or other house space. These are flush doors with sheets of plasterboard or asbestos insulation board behind the facing sheets. For this purpose the door should be fitted with a self-closing fitting.

Doors to outbuildings are usually matchboarded, with boards grooved, tongued and vee jointed, nailed to horizontal ledges and braced with diagonal members. Such doors should be hung with the bottom of the brace on the hinged side so that the brace resists the tendency of the boards to sag.

Doors may have a glazed upper panel or a full length glazed panel, with or without glazing bars.

Exterior doors should have joints put together with a water resistant resin adhesive. Flush doors are made with water soluble adhesives for interior use and water resistant adhesives for exterior use—an important point when ordering.

Some of the door patterns available in softwood, hardwood, plastics and metal

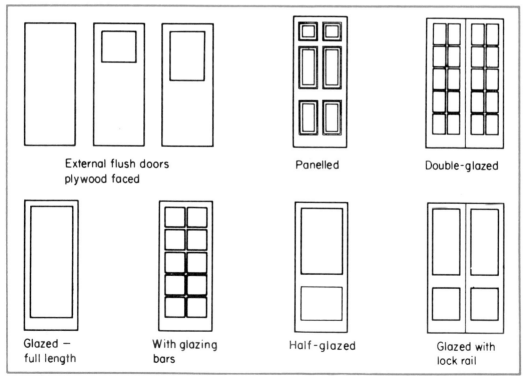

External flush doors plywood faced

Panelled

Double-glazed

Glazed — full length

With glazing bars

Half-glazed

Glazed with lock rail

Aluminium and plastics doors

Aluminium and steel doors are made for houses. Exterior doors of aluminium alloy, with a glazed panel, and complete with an aluminium frame incorporating draught-proof features, are finding favour, but they are costly.

Flush doors faced with plastic, white, coloured or imitation wood grained, are easy to clean and need no painting.

Sliding doors

Where free floor space is limited near a doorway, a sliding door is an advantage. Sliding door gear suitable for light house doors is supplied in packs by several manufacturers, with printed fixing instructions.

Similar gear is suitable for wardrobes. For small cupboard doors there are plastic channels with nylon runners which are easily fixed.

Patio doors and french windows

The traditional French window is inward opening, but most so called French windows in Britain are outward opening and are really glazed casement doors. They may be single or in pairs. If outward opening, metal hooks or friction stays should be fitted to hold them in the open position.

Patio doors, glazed full length and horizontal sliding, are now often preferred to side hung traditional casement doors. Most patio doors advertised are of aluminium alloy framing and track, but they can be of suitable hardwood, specially made. Most local joinery firms will make them to order and they can be hung with suitable sliding door gear.

The aluminium alloy sliding patio doors and windows are weather and draught-proof and need no maintenance other than

Sliding windows and patio doors can be easily adjusted for ventilation, they are draught proof and as they do not swing open they do not obstruct space

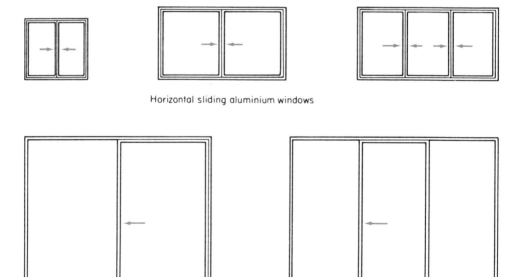

Horizontal sliding aluminium windows

Aluminium patio door/windows

occasional cleaning with soapy water. The full length glass is usually of double glazed insulating units, though single glass doors are also made.

A disadvantage of any full length glazing, from a few inches above floor level upwards, is the risk of injury through accidental collision. It is possible to walk into the glass under the mistaken impression that the door is open. This risk can be diminished by fixing a strip of coloured adhesive tape (the type used for binding carpet and other materials) across the glass at a height of about 900 mm (3 ft) above the floor.

Safety glass, of the type used in car windscreens, has been suggested as the best way to reduce accidental injuries. Some firms supply patio doors fitted with this type of glass.

Door locks and bolts

Locks are of two main types. Mortise locks which are fixed into a mortise or slot cut in the stile of the door (with flush doors which have a hollow core, a lock block is included in manufacture so that a mortise can be cut). Rim locks which are fixed to the inside face of the door. Mortise locks are neater as they are concealed and also give greater security.

There is a wide variety of locks in addition to ordinary types and many have features which greatly improve the strength and resistance to breaking-in. Cylinder locks are fitted partly in a hole drilled through the door but they are essentially rim locks with the main case screwed to the inside and edge of the door.

Bolts are of two main kinds. Most are screwed to the inside face of the door, but there is a mortise type which is fixed into a slot cut in the door and this gives better security as well as a neater appearance.

Cupboards and built-ins

The leading joinery manufacturers stock a standard range of whitewood kitchen units—cupboards, sink units—and also full height cupboard fronts which can be used as door and frame fronts for built-in wardrobes and store cupboards. There is a range of sizes and types and as the cost is relatively low it is hardly worth while making a unit as a one off job, provided you only want plain whitewood for painting.

There are various proprietary ranges of such units in decorative hardwoods and plastic sheet fronts. These are more costly but have a superior finish, which needs little maintenance beyond cleaning.

Where built-ins are to be constructed in the house they can either be made as independent units to fit a given space or,

Using a spirit level-cum-plumb rule to test a vertical surface, preparing for a built-in wardrobe

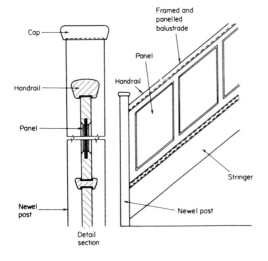

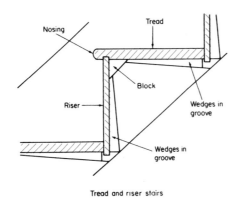

Tread and riser stairs

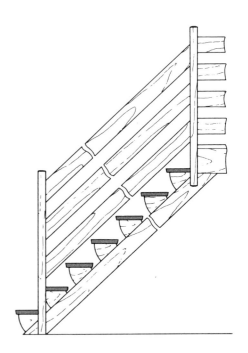

Detail of stair balustrade panelling, handrail and newel post is shown on the left

The treads are supported at the ends in grooves cut in the side stringers, the front of the treads is grooved to take the riser

Below, a typical example of open riser stairs as standardised by one manufacturer. The treads are supported on bracket blocks set into the stringer bearers

where there is an existing wall recess or corner, they can be built piece by piece, using the walls as part of the built-in unit.

Generally, frames 50 mm (2 in) x 38 mm (1½ in) are suitable, with halved joints glued together or plain butt joints secured with proprietary screw blocks (see page 65). Doors can be of blockboard, laminboard or veneered chipboard, cut from a single sheet. Hardboard or plywood on a thin frame can be used but the framing must be sheeted both sides to prevent warping. Alternatively, panelled doors with plywood panels in grooved framing can be used.

Care should be taken to keep all corners truly square. Where a unit is built into a wall recess it may be found that the walls are not perfectly plumb and square, so some packing may be needed.

Staircases

Staircases may be of softwood, hardwood or metal. There are three main types for houses: the tread and riser type with the steps supported at each end on a stringer (a strong board set at the angle of the stairs); the open riser type, with no riser but with a thicker tread to span between the stringers; the spiral type which is usually built around a central newel post.

The standard whitewood staircase made by leading joinery firms for small houses, to suit normal ground floor to ceiling height of 2.43 m (8 ft) plus an additional step formed by the landing, is a tread and riser type. The stringers and balustrades are supported top and bottom of the stairs by jointing to newel posts. Treads and risers are housed in grooves cut in the stringers and are glued and wedged, as illustrated.

The bottom step projects beyond the newel post and the exposed end is curved.

A staircase may be in one straight flight or in two shorter flights with an intermediate landing, turning through 90 degrees or 180 degrees. Where space is restricted winders or tapered steps may be introduced, but these must comply with Building Regulations regarding size and shape.

Open riser staircases are also produced by some joinery firms to their standard design. A typical example is illustrated. They are usually made of hardwood with each tread supported on brackets joined to stout carriage timbers (instead of stringers).

The design of staircases is subject to the requirements of the Building Regulations. The most important are summarised as follows. These are for domestic stairs in a single dwelling.

The pitch angle of the stairs is not more than 42 degrees to the horizontal.

The headroom is not less than 2 m (6 ft 6 in) measured vertically above the pitch line, with a clearance of not less than 1.5 m (5 ft) measured at right angles to the pitch line.

The rise of a step is not more than 220 mm (8½ in); and the going of a step, measured on plan from the nosing of its tread and the nosing of the tread next above it, is not less than 220 mm (8½ in). Obviously you cannot have both the same or the pitch angle would be 45 degrees, whereas the permitted limit is 42 degrees.

In practice a rise of 200 mm (8 in) with a tread of 220 mm (8½ in) is suitable.

With open riser stairs the nosing of the tread of one step must overlap on plan the back edge of the tread of the step below it by not less than 16 mm ($^5/_8$ in).

The stairway must be guarded on each side either by a wall, a secure balustrade, screen or railing not less than 840 mm (2 ft 9 in) measured vertically above the pitch line. For a landing this height must be not less than 900 mm (2 ft 11½ in).

Wood trim and mouldings

Skirtings, architraves or mouldings for trimming doorways or windows, cover strips, picture rails, and small mouldings are called wood trim. They are stocked in a range of patterns and sizes.

Wood trim, such as architraves and small mouldings, is usually fixed to wood backing with small oval or lost head nails. These are punched down and stopped with a filler, then rubbed smooth so that the head is concealed when the work is painted.

Where mouldings or wood strips are fixed direct to block or brick walls, hardened masonry nails or screws and wallplugs may be used.

Skirtings on plastered walls should be supported at the back with wood grounds of the plaster thickness which can be fixed to the wall with masonry nails. The skirting boards can then be nailed to the grounds.

A shrinkage gap may develop between the bottom of a skirting board and a boarded floor. This can be covered with a small quadrant (quarter round) moulding nailed to the floor only—not to the skirting. This leaves it free to move slightly with any further shrinkage.

Chapter 9
Garage doors, fences and gates

After 20 years or so, a close-boarded fence will probably have to be replaced or, at the least, some boards and the arris rails may need renewing. This chapter includes information on close-boarded fences, palings and chain-link fences together with notes on types of post and construction and hanging of gates.

However, we will first start with some brief notes on garage doors.

Garage doors

Garage doors are of two distinct types—wood doors side hung on strap hinges and up-and-over doors of wood, metal or glass fibre reinforced plastic. In addition there are horizontal sliding and folding doors but these are not now much used for domestic garages. Generally, the up-and-over doors are preferred.

Standard wood doors for garages are of two types—boarded on ledged and braced framing, and framed and panelled. They are made in a standard width of 2.134 m (7 ft) and two heights, 2.134 m (7 ft) and 1.981 m (6 ft 6 in). The doors may be completely boarded or panelled or the upper third may be framed and glazed.

Suitable wood frames are supplied to match, of 75 mm x 100 mm (3 in x 4 in) softwood. The feet are fitted with metal dowels for building into the concrete floor.

Up-and-over doors are usually of galvanised steel or aluminium alloy but also of wood and glass-fibre plastic. There are several proprietary types and manufacturers catalogues should be consulted. If possible a visit should be made to the nearest stockist where the doors can be demonstrated. Some doors are spring balanced and some weight balanced. There is a range of widths for single or double car garages. Wider doors are rather heavy and need a strong pull to open and push to close. For a double car garage there is something to be said in favour of two separate single doors with a centre pier or column.

The gear for up-and-over doors is fixed to the side jambs and head of the opening in some cases and to the jamb and roof joists in others. So the type should be chosen to suit the garage construction.

Up-and-over doors of glass fibre reinforced plastic are made in panelled patterns. The mechanism is similar to the metal doors of this type. The material is strong and durable—similar to the plastic material used for moulded boats—and does not need painting.

Door frames

Frames for exterior doors are rebated inside for inward opening and outside for outward opening. Some are made with a sill which may incorporate a steel weather bar, but proprietary metal or plastic weather-tight thresholds are better.

The frame is usually of softwood but hardwood should be used with a hardwood or an aluminium alloy door. The fixing is by ties or lugs screwed to the sides and

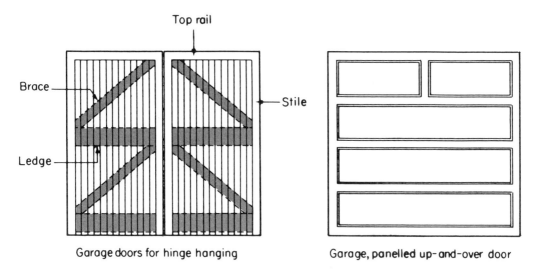

Top rail

Brace

Ledge

Stile

Garage doors for hinge hanging

Garage, panelled up-and-over door

Garage doors are made in various patterns and materials—in wood, metal and plastics. The up-and-over type is generally preferred

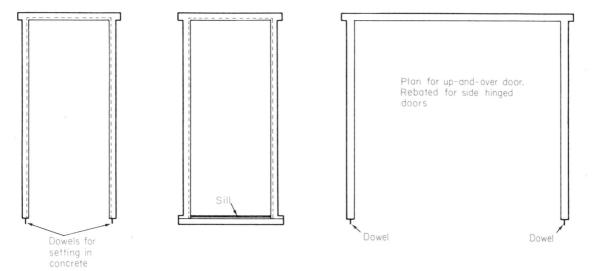

Dowels for setting in concrete

Sill

Plan for up-and-over door. Rebated for side hinged doors

Dowel

Dowel

Wood door frames are rebated for side hinged doors. Draught strip material can be fixed to the rebate and a weatherproof threshold fixed to the sill. Wood sills should be of hardwood

built into the wall jambs. If the frame has no sill the feet are dowelled into the concrete or step.

Interior doors are usually hung to a lining on which a thin strip of wood is nailed to form a door stop. In light partitions rebated frames may be used or linings fixed to timber partition studs (uprights)

Side hung doors may be hung with butt hinges; 100 mm (4 in) for exterior doors, 75 mm (3 in) for interior doors. Each hinge leaf is sunk into the door or frame and fixed with countersunk screws. But there is

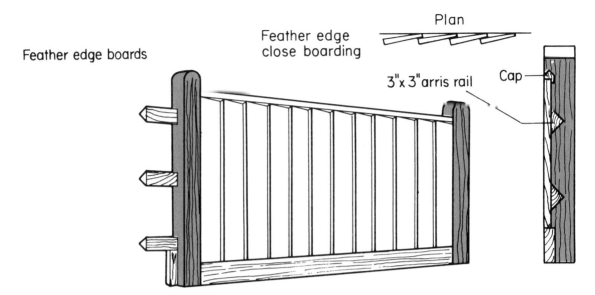

Feather edge boards

Feather edge
close boarding

Plan

3"x 3" arris rail

Cap

Boarded fence. The feather edged boards overlap. Rails can be triangular as shown, or rectangular. The ground board keeps the vertical boarding clear of the ground and helps preservation

a type for which cutting into the door or frame is not required.

Rising hinges can be used to lift the door as it opens and so to clear an adjoining floor covering.

Fences

Fences may be ornamental or protective, or both. If you want to keep out dogs and cats you need either close boarding or close chain link. The fence should be fairly high to prevent animals jumping over it. If you want to keep out intruders you need a high strong fence, but it need not be close boarded. A fence of either palings, rails or strong chain link mesh is perhaps better than close boarding which conceals the intruder.

Under Planning Regulations the height of front fences—those in front of the building line—is limited to 1.2 m (4 ft) and to 2.1 m (7 ft) for side and rear fences. In order to make the rear of the premises

difficult for intruders to enter you must have a high fence and side gate to close the gaps at the side or sides of a semi-detached or detached house. If you feel there are special reasons why you should be allowed to have higher fences than mentioned above you can apply for planning permission.

There is a very wide range of materials, patterns and systems of fencing and gates, in timber, steel, plastic and pre-cast concrete.

Post and wire fences are suitable if you intend growing a hedge. Wired cleft chestnut fences give better protection against animals.

Interwoven softwood slat fences in panels for fixing between posts are cheaper than boarded fences but less durable. They are rather easily damaged and then tend to go to pieces.

A better type of panelled fence is that of thin larch weatherboarding on a light framing. Larch has good resistance to decay. These panels are prefabricated, like the interwoven type, and are fixed between posts simply by nailing.

Boarded fencing of the traditional type consists of posts, rails and vertical boards, which are feather edged for nailing to the rails. The fencing can be sawn to length from suitable timber or bought in kit form ready for erection. The boards are fixed to overlap slightly.

Durability is an important factor in fencing, so it is worth some extra cost to choose decay resistant timbers—oak, larch or Western red cedar.

If a softwood—a fir or pine wood—is used, it must be obtained pressure impregnated with preservative if it is to last any length of time. Brush treatment with a preservative is effective for a year or two but must be renewed regularly to prevent decay.

Protection

The most vulnerable parts of a timber fence are those in or close to the ground. Post stumps especially need protection. Softwood posts should have a few holes drilled diagonally from a few inches above ground level downwards. These should be filled with preservative, using a funnel, and refilled when the first dose has soaked into the timber. The holes can then be plugged with cork or piece of wood. The treatment can be renewed every few years.

Vertical boarding should not be allowed to touch the ground. A horizontal ground board should be fixed to the posts, nailing it to wood fillets at the post sides. The vertical boarding then terminates on top of the ground board. If the ground board rots it can easily be removed and replaced with new.

Posts

Pre-cast concrete posts are the best for durability. They can be obtained slotted to take timber rails. Short concrete stumps are also available for repairs to decayed

timber posts. The decayed stump is sawn off above ground and holes drilled higher up so that the concrete stump can be bolted to the timber.

In soft ground posts should be concreted into the ground, with about 12 mm (6 in) of concrete all round and underneath, and the top of the concrete brought above ground and finished by trowelling to an outward slope. A 1:2:4 cement-lime-sand mix (see page 4) is quite strong enough.

In strong ground, such as sandy gravel, the posts can be wedged in at the bottom with a few bricks and the hole then filled with the soil, well rammed.

High boarded fences should have extra support against strong winds by fixing diagonal struts to every second or third post.

A saddleback capping on top of the boards is advisable to protect them from rain and also to add to appearance. The wood posts, too, should be capped, either with bevelled wood caps or metal (lead, zinc, aluminium). These caps should be cut at the corners and turned down about 25 mm (1 in) and nailed along the edges with rustless nails.

All nails used in fencing should be galvanised steel or, better still, aluminium alloy.

Horizontal boarding can be used instead of vertical and if thick enough—not less than 16 mm ($^5/_8$ in)—horizontal rails are not needed. The boards can be nailed to wood fillets on the sides of the posts. Alternatively the boards can be nailed on the face of the posts but it is then desirable to have boards long enough to span two bays, with the ends staggered on alternate posts.

Palings

Rail and pale fences look good and are particularly suitable for front boundary

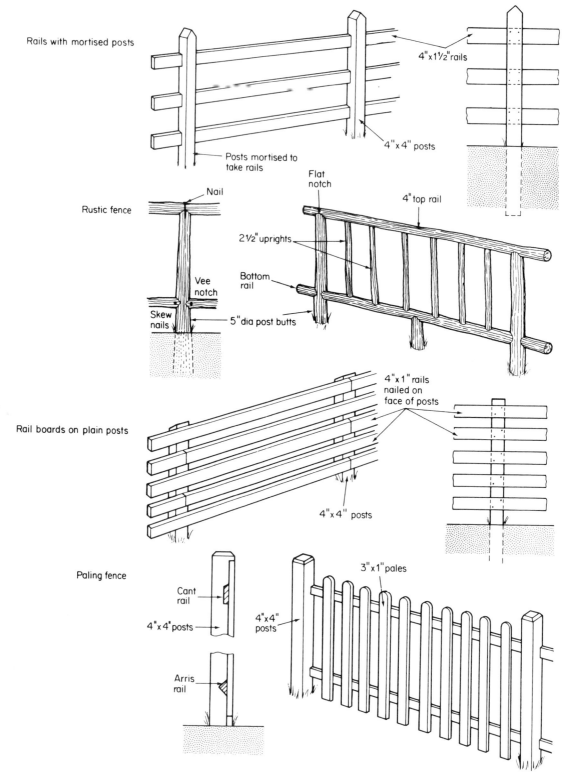

Rails with mortised posts

4"x1½" rails

4"x4" posts

Posts mortised to take rails

Rustic fence

Nail

Flat notch

4" top rail

2½" uprights

Bottom rail

Vee notch

Skew nails

5" dia post butts

Rail boards on plain posts

4"x1" rails nailed on face of posts

4"x4" posts

Paling fence

Cant rail

3"x1" pales

4"x4" posts

4"x4" posts

Arris rail

Fences of open types with railings and palings. Posts should preferably be of oak, or larch. If rustic material is used the bark should be stripped

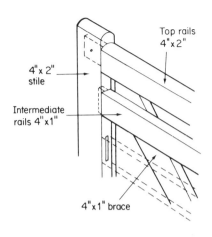

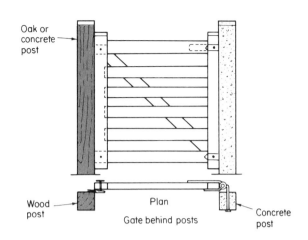

A typical garden gate of wood—preferably of hardwood. The rails are tenoned into the vertical stiles. Posts preferably of oak or pre-cast concrete

fencing, using either sawn timber treated with preservative or planed and painted wood. Several types are available.

The pales should be 75 mm x 18 mm (3 in x ¾ in), with 75 mm (3 in) spaces between. With posts spaced at 2 m (6 ft 6 in) centres the railes can be 100 mm x 50 mm (4 in x 2 in) fixed through mortise slots cut in the posts.

Post and rail fence

This is a rural type fence, usually of oak or elm. Posts are usually 100 mm x 100 mm (4 in x 4 in) with 100 mm x 50 mm (4 in x 2 in) rails fixed through mortise slots in the posts.

Fencing kits, as already mentioned, are offered by several firms. These include some special types, such as louvred fences in which boards are fixed, either vertically or horizontally at 45 degrees. This forms a screen which allows air to pass through but obstructs vision.

Metal railings

There are many types of metal railings from the severely practical chain link mesh, attached to posts of pre-cast reinforced concrete or of tubular steel, to ornamental fencing of straight and curved mild steel bars and rods.

Ornamental metal fences are best set on a low brick or block wall. The fences are supplied in sections with lugs for building into the supporting wall and also at the sides for building into piers.

Plastics fencing

Sectional fencing is made in durable plastic material, with posts and rails of box or hollow section. They are rot proof and do not need decorating.

With reasonable treatment this type of fence may be expected to last well, but any damage may be difficult to repair.

Gates

Gates may be of either wood or metal. The wood types include close-boarded with feather edged boards overlapping. Rail and pale with open spaces between the pales and various ornamental patterns. The gates are framed with mortise and tenon joints.

The joints should be put together either in thick gloss paint or a water resistant adhesive, and the tenons should be secured with pegs. A simple type of gate is illustrated on page 83.

Gates of rot resistant woods—oak, larch, Western red cedar, elm—or one of the more durable imported hardwoods, should be treated with a preservative of suitable colour to maintain the appearance as well as to give extra protection.

Metal gates are made in a wide variety. Manufacturers issue illustrated catalogues and fixing instructions.

Strong posts, fixed into the ground by concreting, are essential to prevent the post on the hanging side from moving by the pull of the gate. Oak or other durable hardwood or concrete posts 150 mm x 150 mm (6 in x 6 in) is recommended.

Brick or block piers can be used instead of posts. They should be at least a brick-and-half square for single gates and two-brick square for double gates.

Care should be taken to set out a straight line of fencing by stretching a string line end to end. Intermediate post positions should be marked with pegs. Rail ends should meet at posts.

On sloping ground the fence sections should be stepped and each section levelled.

Gate posts should be positioned to give the correct clearances for hinges and fastener.

Chapter 10
Small timber buildings

Small timber sheds, home workshops, conservatories, verandahs and porches are made by many firms in prefabricated sections for erection on a concrete or paved base/foundation. They are simple to erect, but if you prefer to build from basic materials there is nothing difficult about the construction. Follow the jointing methods described in Chapters 7 and 8.

Constructing a shed/workshop

The design for a shed or workshop (which could have a variety of uses) illustrated is 2.35 m (7 ft 9 in) wide over the frames. It may be of any reasonable length but for most purposes 3 m (10 ft) will be suitable.

The construction is substantial, of timber, preferably planed, with horizontal shiplap boards on 50 mm x 50 mm (2 in x 2 in) upright studs and horizontal rails with 75 mm x 38 mm (3 in x 1½ in) rafters and 75 mm x 50 mm (3 in x 2 in) sill plates and corner posts.

A standard wood casement window and a ledged, braced and boarded door can be

Shed/workshop/playroom/summer house. The construction is fairly simple. Weather boards or asbestos-cement sheets for exterior cladding. Any suitable standard window and door can be used (see page 86 for plan)

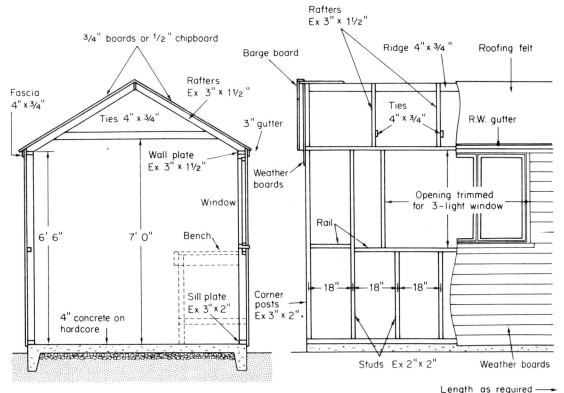

Cross section   Side

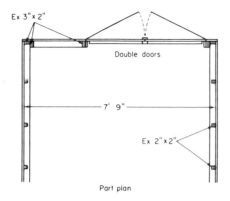

Ex 3" x 2"

Double doors

7' 9"

Ex 2" x 2"

Part plan

The shed/workshop shown in the previous illustration in section and elevation is here in part plan. Sides and front and back can be made in sections. See page 62 for simple joints

nailed to the frames. Any suitable size and pattern of window and door can be selected. It is advisable to coat the sides of the window and door frames with thick gloss paint shortly before fixing them. This will seal the junction and prevent interior decay.

The base floor can be of concrete 100 mm (4 in) thick on a level bed of hardcore, with the perimeter trenched down below ground level. The overall size of the base should be the same as that of the bare framing, so that the lower edge of the boards will stand clear of the concrete base and allow rainwater to run off.

The framing consists of studs (uprights) and rails (horizontals). You can make halved joints where they meet, but nailing with 50 mm (2 in) nails will stiffen the whole structure. The boards should be 12 mm (½ in) rebated shiplap section for horizontal fixing. For vertical fixing, tongued and grooved vee jointed section of the same thickness can be used.

An alternative to boards of natural wood is tempered hardboard (see page 61); ordinary hardboard is not suitable. Tempered hardboard is denser and better resistant to damp but it must be protected by painting. Alternatively, you can use flat asbestos-cement sheets, but these are brittle and will not stand hard knocks.

The roof can be boarded with sawn boards 12 mm (½ in) thick or with 19 mm (¾ in) chipboard. This should be covered with a good quality mineral-surfaced bituminous roofing felt.

A fascia board should be nailed all along each end of the roof and a plastic rainwater gutter and downpipe fixed along the front. The pipe can terminate above a rainwater butt or be connected to an underground pitch fibre pipe leading into a soak-away sump (a hole in the ground filled with rubble).

The boarding can be painted—primer, undercoat and gloss coat. Alternatively, a preservative can be brushed on, with a renewal coat every two or three years.

To prevent damp rising through the concrete base-floor, a layer of thick polythene should be laid over the hardcore before placing the concrete. The timber bottom rail of the framing should be given two coats of bitumen paint or emulsion before fixing as this will inevitably be in a damp position in wet weather.

A structure of this kind makes a substantial shed for storage, a home workshop, a playroom, or, with a pair of casement doors, a summer house.

If you want it to be used in winter with some form of heating it should be insulated. The simplest way to do this is to back the boarding between the frames with 12 mm (½ in) expanded polystyrene sheets. Alternatively, nail foil-backed plasterboard sheets on to the inside face of the frame.

Building a conservatory

A conservatory can be added to a house or bungalow without interfering much with the existing structure. There are many prefabricated types advertised and these are fairly simple to erect on a prepared concrete base-floor. If you prefer to build from basic

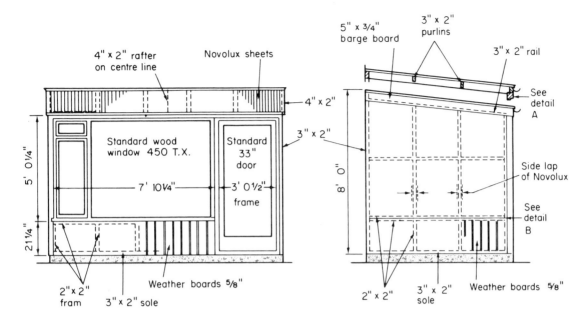

4" x 2" rafter on centre line
Novolux sheets
4" x 2"
5' 0¼"
Standard wood window 450 T.X.
Standard 33" door
7' 10¼"
3' 0½" frame
3" x 2"
21¼"
2" x 2" fram
3" x 2" sole
Weather boards ⅝"

5" x ¾" barge board
3" x 2" purlins
3" x 2" rail
See detail A
8' 0"
Side lap of Novolux
See detail B
2" x 2"
3" x 2" sole
Weather boards ⅝"

A conservatory using a large standard window, door and frame for the front with corrugated plastics sheeting on a wood frame for the sides. (Where one side is close to a boundary it must be of brickwork or blockwork to comply with Building Regulations)

materials, the design illustrated is suitable. The construction is simplified by making use of a standard wood window and casement door.

The plinth wall can be of 75 mm x 50 mm (3 in x 2 in) planed softwood framing, with external horizontal shiplap or vertical tongued and grooved boarding, as described for the shed-workshop. The inside of this framing can be lined with foil-backed plasterboard.

The plinth frame should be bolted down to the concrete base/floor, which should be 100 mm (4 in) thick.

Anchor bolts are best but coach bolts are suitable if a large washer is placed against the round head so that it gives a good hold in the concrete. The bolts can be cast into the concrete at intervals of about 600 mm (2 ft), with the bottom plate drilled to correspond.

The finished floor should be at least 100 mm (4 in) above the ground level. The surface soil should be stripped first and a bed of hardcore levelled and consolidated, then blinded with sand to provide a smooth surface for a dampproof membrane of thick polythene.

The underside of the frame plate should be given two coats of bituminous paint before fixing. Alternatively, a strip of bituminous felt can be laid as a dampproof course.

The front of the conservatory consists of a standard wood casement window (a choice can be made of the many patterns and sizes available), with a glazed door and frame placed against the frame and screwed to it.

The sides of the structure may be framed and clad with Novolux corrugated sheets, or with weather boarding.

Corner posts are 75 mm x 50 mm (3 in x 2 in) nominal, but planed down to the same depth as the window and door frames. A door strip can be nailed to the posts each side of the door to form a rebated frame. Alternatively, a standard door frame can be used, extending it at the top to form a fixed light over the doorway.

The roof can be framed with purlins and supporting rafters to be covered with corrugated translucent plastic sheets. The standard sheets with 75 mm (3 in corruga-tions, such as Novolux, can be fixed with the drive screws and plastic washers to purlins spaced up to 900 mm (3 ft) centres. The cheaper plastic sheets with small corrugations are not recommended for permanent roofing.

The window frame can be screwed to the posts and the sills screwed to the timber plinth. (A brick or block plinth wall can be built if preferred; in this case the window frames should be secured to the wall with anchor bolts set in cement mortar.)

A boarded and felted roof, similar to that described for the shed-workshop, with the addition of a plasterboard or insulating board ceiling, will give much better thermal insulation. If the conservatory is mainly for plants it should be remembered that this type of roof will, of course, reduce the daylight.

Verandahs

A verandah may be open or enclosed. The open type consists of a flat or lean-to roof supported on posts. It may extend the full width of the rear wall of the house or bungalow. Where a corner space exists between the back of the garage and the house, it may cover the corner and so give shelter between the rear garage door and the kitchen door.

The construction is mainly similar to the conservatory described above.

The posts for an open verandah should be secured to the concrete foundation (or, in the case of a verandah on a raised terrace, to the brick retaining wall) by a galvanised steel or a copper dowel inserted in the foot of the post and set in a concrete base.

To prevent rot attacking the foot of the post the end grain should be coated with two coats gloss or bituminous paint—one

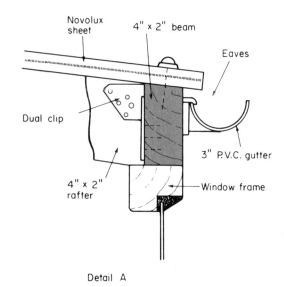

Detail A

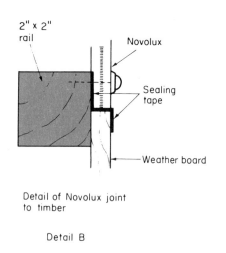

Detail of Novolux joint to timber

Detail B

Detail of fixings for the Novolux sheeting to roof and side for the conservatory shown in the illustration on page 87

cost before the dowel is fixed and another after, including the dowel.

The raised base or stool should be of fine concrete with small grit aggregate of a stiff mix. It can be built up in layers, allowing the inner layer to partly set and then applying the final layer. This can be done after the post has been erected and temporarily supported with struts.

The front beam can then be bolted to

the post heads. The roof frame can be constructed with purlins supported on main rafters. In the section shown in the diagram the main rafters are supported against the house wall on a timber plate fixed to the wall with expanding shell bolts (Rawlbolts). The front ends are cut to fit over the front beam and then skew nailed.

Small section fillets are screwed to the sides of the rafters and the purlin ends are cut to fit over these. Alternatively, metal fastening plates can be used.

With purlins at not more than 900 mm (3 ft) centres the roof can be covered with corrugated sheets—the large 75 mm (3 in) profile, as described for the conservatory.

Chapter 11
Plastering and rendering

The term plastering is confined to interior work on walls and ceilings. Rendering is the usual term describing external cement mixes applied as a finish to walls of common bricks or blocks.

Plastering is not an easy craft for a beginner and for most purposes it is advisable to line walls and ceilings with a dry finish—plasterboard or other wallboard. These are briefly described in Chapter 7.

Plastering on walls

Modern plasters are produced from gypsum. There are several types, from plaster of Paris which sets within a minute or so and is useless except for spot repairs, to the general purpose gypsum plasters which are retarded in setting to give you time to apply and finish the surface.

For most purposes two-coat plastering on brick or block walls is sufficient, though a better finish is obtainable with three coats, especially if the wall has a very irregular surface. Any depressions in the wall can be filled with a mix of cement-lime-sand in the proportions of 1:2:9. A strong cement mix is not suitable for this as it would shrink and crack.

The equipment needed consists of a mixing board about 1 m (3 ft 3 in) square, a clean bucket, a trestle or table, a plumb line and bob, a straightedge batten 2 m (7 ft)

long, and a hawk. The latter is a piece of board about 250 mm (10 in) square with a handle underneath. You can carry a small supply of plaster on it, holding the hawk in one hand while you apply the plaster with the other.

Plaster is applied with a rectangular steel or aluminium plastering trowel about 225 mm X 100 mm (9 in X 4 in).

For small jobs it is advisable to buy general purpose plaster, but ask for a copy of the manufacturer's printed instructions. The plaster must be kept dry while stored.

Mixing

Place the dry plaster powder on a board about 1 m (3 ft) square, scoop a hollow in the middle of the heap and apply water through the rose of a watering can, while a helper mixes it with a trowel.

Take up some plaster on the hawk, tilt it towards you as you work so that you can take it up a trowelfull at a time.

Start plastering at the bottom of the wall and sweep it upwards with the trowel, to a thickness of about 12 mm ($\frac{1}{2}$ in) for the undercoat. The surface should be left fairly straight but not perfectly smoothed.

On a wall you should first nail wood screeding battens of 1.8 m (6 ft), plumbing them vertically up the wall. Alternatively, you can form the screeds in plaster, using a straightedge to true the surface.

Whichever method is used, when the plaster has been applied between the screeds, and whilst it is still soft, the straightedge must be moved over the screeds to level off the plaster. When this has nearly set the screed battens (if you used these) can be removed and the gaps made good with plaster.

Before the undercoat sets, but has firmed, it must be scratched to form a good key for the finishing coat. A scratcher can be made with a short length of wood batten, with a handle nailed to one side, and six 2 in nails driven through the batten piece. Scratch the surface of the plaster, but not deeply.

When the undercoat has set and dried, the finishing coat can be applied with the trowel, starting at the bottom and sweeping upwards. The should finish about 2 mm thick. The surface should be ironed smooth but this must be done before final setting of the plaster.

Ceilings

The traditional method of lathing ceiling joists was to nail wood laths with small gaps between to the joints. This method is now obsolete.

Gypsum lathboard—a type of plaster-board—is nailed on with 38 mm (1½ in) rustless nails, leaving a gap between the sides of the boards. A strip of scrim fabric should be set in plaster at the angle between the wall and the lathboard, as reinforcement to prevent cracking at this point.

It will be understood that the ceilings should be done before the wall plastering and the scrim set at the corner before the ceiling undercoat is applied.

Plastering, especially on ceilings, is hard, as well as skilled, work. Try your hand on a small area before tackling a full-size room.

Thermal insulation of ceilings

For ceilings under the roof of a bungalow or the top rooms of a house, a high degree of thermal insulation is required. At least 76 mm (3 in) of glass fibre quilting is required, or other material with equivalent thermal insulation. Official regulations may increase this thickness in the near future. Experts advise 100 mm (4 in) at least, but in Northern Europe at least 177 mm (7 in) is standard.

There are two types of glass fibre and mineral wool, one 450 mm (18 in) wide, in rolls, for placing between ceiling joists; the other 1.8 m (6 ft) blanket material for draping over the joists.

Mineral wool loose fill, supplied in bags, can be poured into the space between the joists.

External rendering

Renderings of cement mixes on external walls should be of moderate strength or, for sheltered positions, of rather low strength. Very strong mixes, such as 1 cement to 3 sand by volume, are liable to shrink and crack on large areas.

For ordinary brickwork or blockwork a mix of 1 cement, 1 hydrated powder lime and 5 to 6 parts washed sand is suitable. The wall surface should be clean and, if smooth, the joints should be raked out and smooth faced blocks should be punched or hacked to afford a key for the rendering.

Although one-coat rendering may suffice, it is liable to allow the joint lines to show through. Two-coat work which consists of an undercoat 12 mm (½ in) thick and a finishing coat 7 mm to 9 mm (average ¼ in or a little more) is advisable.

The finish should be scraped with the edge of the trowel or textured by dabbing with a coarse cloth or by using a wood comb or one of the special tools made for the purpose.

A smoothly trowelled finish is undesirable as it tends to show fine crazing or cracks.

Roughcast and pebbledash

Roughcast finish consists of a wet mix of the same proportion as the undercoat with the addition of sand and crushed stone or gravel, about 7 mm to 12 mm, (average about $\frac{3}{8}$ in). It is thrown on with a scoop and makes a durable finish.

Pebbledash consists of small pebbles or crushed stone, graded in sizes as for rough-cast, but thrown on dry to be embedded in the undercoat while this is still soft. It is advisable to add pressure with a trowel or wood block to make sure of good adhesion. This makes a very durable finish which sheds rainwater easily.

Special coloured mixes are obtainable for application with a hand machine—the Tyrolean finish is one. This throws the wet mix on by turning a handle.

Appendix

Useful addresses

The following are some of the leading firms manufacturing materials and components widely used in house building. Addresses are of the head office or factory but they have main supply depots throughout Britain. These can be found in most of the yellow page telephone directories.

The Building Centre, London, can also provide information on all manufacturers of specific products.

Bricks

London Brick Co., Africa House, Kingsway, London WC.

Blocks, lightweight, load bearing, insulation

Thermalite Ytong Ltd., Lea Marston, Sutton Coldfield, Warwickshire.

Joinery

Boulton & Paul (Joinery) Ltd., Riverside Works, Norwich, Norfolk.
Magnet Joinery Ltd., Keighley, Yorkshire.
Sharp Bros & Knight Ltd., Burton-on-Trent, Staffs.

Roofing tiles

Marley Roofing, Sevenoaks, Kent.
Redland Tiles Ltd., Castle Gate, Reigate, Surrey.

Floorings

Marley Floor Tile Co. Ltd., London Road, Riverhead, Sevenoaks, Kent.

Concrete slabs, blocks and prefabricated products

Marley Concrete Ltd., Peasmarsh, Guildford, Surrey.

Corrugated plastic sheets

I.C.I. Novolux, Hyde, Cheshire.

Catalogues or brochures are available from most of the above.

Index

FOR YOUR REFERENCE

A great deal of time can be saved if you have at your fingertips information concerning the quantities, prices and sources of supply you will need. It will also ensure that you order the amount you require.

Use the following pages to keep an accurate account of materials you will require for the specific job—garden paths of concrete or brick, garden walls, patios, garage, shed or small buildings, etc.

If you require space for additional information use the back cover.

JOB:

Tools required:

Tools required from hire shop:

Tool	*Period of hire*	*Cost per day/week*

Amount of material required:

Cost of materials (obtain quotes from two or three firms):

Estimated time to be allowed for job:

JOB:

Tools required:

Tools required from hire shop:

Tool	Period of hire	Cost per day/week

Amount of material required:

Cost of materials (obtain quotes from two or three firms):

Estimated time to be allowed for job:

JOB:

Tools required:

Tools required from hire shop:

Tool	*Period of hire*	*Cost per day/week*

Amount of material required:

Cost of materials (obtain quotes from two or three firms):

Estimated time to be allowed for job:

JOB:

Tools required:

Tools required from hire shop:

Tool	*Period of hire*	*Cost per day/week*

Amount of material required:

Cost of materials (obtain quotes from two or three firms):

Estimated time to be allowed for job:

JOB:

Tools required:

Tools required from hire shop:

Tool   *Period of hire*   *Cost per day/week*

Amount of material required:

Cost of materials (obtain quotes from two or three firms):

Estimated time to be allowed for job:

JOB:

Tools required:

Tools required from hire shop:

Tool	Period of hire	Cost per day/week

Amount of material required:

Cost of materials (obtain quotes from two or three firms):

Estimated time to be allowed for job:

JOB:

Tools required:

Tools required from hire shop:

Tool   *Period of hire*   *Cost per day/week*

Amount of material required:

Cost of materials (obtain quotes from two or three firms):

Estimated time to be allowed for job: